THROUGH THE
FRENCH PROVINCES

Carcassonne

THROUGH THE FRENCH PROVINCES

BY
ERNEST PEIXOTTO

ILLUSTRATIONS BY THE AUTHOR

NEW AND REVISED EDITION

CHARLES SCRIBNER'S SONS
NEW YORK · LONDON
1928

TO MY WIFE

FOR WHOM FRANCE
HAS EVER BEEN A SOURCE OF INSPIRATION
THIS BOOK
IS AFFECTIONATELY INSCRIBED

PREFACE TO THE NEW EDITION

THE first edition of this book was published nearly twenty years ago and met with a very favorable reception. The demand for it ever since has been deemed sufficient, in the opinion of its publishers, to warrant the issue of a new edition. But to this its author would only consent on condition that the book should be carefully revised and rewritten at least in part so as to bring it more or less up to date, as many things have happened in France since these pages were first printed.

I have, therefore, recently revisited most of the places described and have completely rewritten certain chapters and added some entirely new material, so that, as it now stands, "Through the French Provinces" is almost a new book. It may, therefore, very well serve as a sort of guide to leisurely motorists and travellers who have the time and inclination to hunt up quaint and interesting places, near the beaten track, to be sure, but usually entirely overlooked by the more hurried tourist.

PREFACE

YEARS ago, when I went as a mere boy to study in France, the country and its picturesque towns and villages took a strong hold upon me. Since then, despite repeated sojourns and years of travel, the French provinces seem ever to unfold new riches and to prove an inexhaustible mine of interest. With the possible exception of Italy, I know of no country whose little towns so well repay investigation, and yet, until recent years of automobiling, how little have they been visited by the tourist!

If the succeeding pages serve to open new vistas to the careful traveller—to the lover of the picturesque or the student of architecture—and bring to his notice some hitherto unknown corners of an altogether fascinating country, the purpose of this book will have been fulfilled.

The writer wishes to thank the friends in France who have contributed so much to the pleasure of these journeys and made so many of their most agreeable features possible.

CONTENTS

[xi]

CONTENTS

LIST OF ILLUSTRATIONS

LIST OF ILLUSTRATIONS

LIST OF ILLUSTRATIONS

THE CHARM OF THE FRENCH
PROVINCES

THE CHARM OF THE FRENCH PROVINCES

C AN any one who really knows them, fail to feel the charm of the French Provinces— and not alone their charm, but their beauty and their infinite variety? And yet, until recent years and the more general use of the motor, they were (and in many ways are still, for that matter) almost a terra incognita to the average tourist. He visits Vichy, to be sure, or Aix-les-Bains or the smiling beaches of Deauville and Dinard, or the rocky coast at Biarritz. But what have these places, with their blatant casinos, their huge caravansaries and their cosmopolitan throngs, to do with "la belle terre de France"; with the rare charm of the real French countryside?

Since the War, however, tourist agencies have sprung up who plan pleasant journeys in sight-seeing cars (or in luxurious private limousines) to places of interest round about Paris, to the "châteaux country"

THROUGH THE FRENCH PROVINCES

and even farther afield, but these companies, for the most part, plan their trips to suit the hurried tourist.

This book, on the other hand, is intended for him who would be a more leisurely traveler, who has the time and the inclination to see not only the things that lie along the beaten track, but also to digress, and take, now and then, a country road instead of the broad highway; to stop for a night occasionally in the modest inn of a provincial town and to enjoy at times the thrill that comes with a sense of discovery.

And what a reward there is in France for such a traveler! If he loves the purely picturesque, he can espy castles on crags; he can discover quaint villages nestled in verdant valleys or perched on steep hill-tops diapered, like Oriental carpets, with multicoloured fields. If he loves nature unadorned, he can find mountains and wild valleys, waterfalls in rocky gorges, grottos hung with stalactites, underground rivers, and mysterious caverns where prehistoric man once dwelt. Or, if he is interested in art or in architecture, he can discover each day at least one church or town hall or château to enthrall him.

The Gothic houses of Touraine, built of the fine white limestone of Montrichard; the golden *mas* of

He can espy castles on crags

Provence, resembling the Spanish casita; the chalets of the Vosges and the Pyrenees, with their broad overhanging roofs; the sturdy peasant houses of Lorraine; the thatched farms and slate-roofed manor-houses of Normandy; the stone huts and calvaries of Brittany; the massive military monuments of the Middle Ages; the incomparable châteaux that the Renaissance and the Grand Siécle have left; the great cathedrals that have no equals in the world—all these lie ready at the choice of the judicious traveler in France, if he but knows where to go and what he wants to see.

For France, though a small country not as large as the State of Texas, is so varied in climate and in its physical aspect, that its provinces present an infinite variety, each region having a character quite its own. The apple orchards and smiling half-timbered cottages of Normandy; the wild reaches of the Causses, the great plains of the Beauce and Brie, the wooded valleys and lakes of the Vosges, the dark mountains of Auvergne and the brilliant sunshine of Provence; the rocky hemicycles of the Jura, the grandeur of the Pyrenees and the Alps of Savoy; the calm beauty of the Basque region—all these are cited as but a few

[5]

examples of the diversity of the French landscape
that has served as a source of inspiration to all the
modern schools of painting. Even the rivers present
a similar variety: the smiling meanders of the Seine
or Marne contrasting with the dark gorges of the Lot
and Dordogne; the sylvan banks of the slow-winding
Yonne so different from the rocky shores of the roar-
ing Rhone.

Man himself, too, his clothes and his customs, are
scarcely less diversified, for the people of France are
still rebellious to Babbitry and standardization.
From the silent Breton, dressed in black, and the
canny Norman in his blue smock, to the volatile son
of the Midi—what contrasts and what a variety of
types to be encountered and studied!

The Great War has left little or no outward trace
upon the people or their country, except in the in-
vaded regions. But please note that I say *outward*
sign. An occasional billeting sign, or, along the old
S. O. S., a wooden diamond-shaped square marked
"Slow Danger Curve," or a long, thin line of tele-
graph-poles spreading their broad arms so differently
from the usual French equipment and still stenciled
with the cabalistic letters: U. S. A., S. C., are all that

the American might note to remind him of the War. But in its inner life, in the very essence of its soul,

What a variety of types!

France has been deeply affected by the Great War. Hardly a family but has its tragedy. Hardly a family but feels the pinch of taxes, of the high cost of living, of burdens and cares that it never knew nor even dreamt of prior to 1914. But, to the traveler, these cares and sorrows are not apparent, for, notwithstanding much that has been said to the contrary, the French are a proud and reserved people and usually keep their troubles hidden within the bosom of their own families.

The roads of France also (and this is of capital importance to the motorist) now show very little sign of the shock of war. During four long years, they were called upon to carry, not alone the weight of all the allied armies, but of their equipment and supplies as well. Down even as far as Bordeaux and Dijon, three-ton trucks went pounding and thundering along in never-ending processions, while all through northern France, artillery, men, supplies were being constantly rushed from one threatened point to another. Not only the top-soil of the roads vanished in clouds of dust, but even the solid rock road-beds themselves were sorely shaken. Careful and patient toil however, combined with good engineering, have now, little by little, repaired these ravages, so that the main highways, the great *Routes Nationales* that traverse France in all directions, now stretch, remade and freshly tarred, like long blue-black ribbons, under their double and sometimes quadruple lines of trees, that rise to vast overarching branches, which close overhead like the lofty vaults of some great cathedral, the outer rows resembling aisles, through whose moving boles, as one motors along, one catches fleeting glimpses of exquisitely finished landscapes framed as in the windows of a Gothic nave.

These national roads that radiate like arteries in every direction from the heart of France, which is Paris, feed and are fed by less important byways, more tortuous, more hilly, but often much more interesting than the main routes themselves. And one should not hesitate, at times, to investigate these lesser roads for they are apt to lead to spots of unexpected beauty, nature often reserving for them her most alluring pictures.

Along them too, one comes upon the "hostelleries" that have become such a modern feature of traveling in France. These wayside inns have sprung up like mushrooms by the roadside, sometimes installed in an humble farmhouse, freshly painted and bedecked with gay flowers and parasols; sometimes lodged in a huge château (O, decadence des grandeurs!) and named for some King's favorite; sometimes in an ancient abbey or an old mill nestled beside a trout-stream. Though undoubtedly attractive, these inns are not always good in spite of their high prices but, if this be the case, they can usually be replaced by a more "serious" hotel in the town near by.

In general, I think it may safely be said that the hotels in France have greatly improved since the War in what is termed by the French "confort moderne," which is to say that there is more and better plumbing, that steam heat has been installed and that clean, simply furnished rooms have almost entirely replaced the old-fashioned bedrooms with their stuffy, dingy hangings and curtains.

But one sighs, alas, for the pre-War cuisine, for the good things under which the table of a provincial hotel used to groan. And one remembers, with a sigh, the delicacies and the sauces, the game and the patties, that seldom, if ever, grace the menus nowadays.

There is no doubt of it, however, France is still a very pleasant place to live in—as I think I have a right to say, who pass a part of every year in it. Situated neither too far to the north nor too far to the

Rouen from the Faubourg of Saint Sever

south, it enjoys a fine, temperate climate, its people are kindly and eminently humane, and its territory, as I have already endeavored to point out, is so diversified with natural beauties and so enhanced by the handiwork of man, that this very *embarras de choix* makes it difficult for one to choose an itinerary and to decide what to see or what to describe.

The usual Anglo-Saxon traveler debarks at one of the Channel ports and proceeds thence up to Paris. He seldom lingers on the way, but if he does, he can find much to interest him. Between Cherbourg and the capital lie Bayeux and Coutances, and, with a little détour, Mont St. Michel and its fascinating surroundings. If, on the other hand, he debarks at Havre, he can break his journey at picturesque Caudebec and at Rouen that most fascinating of Norman towns, whose tall church spires overshadow its narrow streets of Gothic houses, many of which saw the Maid as she passed between their timbered façades. Or, again, he may stop at Les Andelys, where the ruins of Cœur de Lion's castle mirror themselves in the quiet waters of the Seine, or, for that matter, at a half dozen other places of interest. But Normandy and Brittany would demand a book unto themselves

Tall church spires overshadow its narrow streets

and have, besides, been presented to English-speaking tourists in a number of excellent volumes.

So, for the purposes of this book, let us start from Paris southward, bear off to the west, and explore some of the out-of-the-way corners almost down to the Pyrenees.

UNFREQUENTED CHATEAUX NEAR FONTAINEBLEAU

UNFREQUENTED CHATEAUX
NEAR FONTAINEBLEAU

MELUN is but a short hour southward from Paris either by train or motor-car, on the northern confines of the Forest of Fontainebleau, and the stags, pursued by the pack of baying hounds, often make their last stand in the Bois de la Rochette which adjoins Melun to the south.

Should you alight from the train in autumn at about four o'clock, you would surely wonder, as you glanced at the long provincial street with its single trolley tracks, why so goodly an array of handsome traps and motor cars were drawn up before the station, and why so smart a crowd of footmen stood anxiously scanning the crowd for the master's familiar face. Presently the carriages would whisk off in different directions, some down under the railroad bridge toward Vives-Eaux and Fortoiseau, some up the long street and out over the plains to the north toward Vaux-Praslin, others to follow along the banks of the Seine to La Rochette on one side or Vaux-le-Pénil on the other.

Did you take one of these carriages sent six miles across country by some kind host to meet you, you would now follow the clear white road up over the plateau, skirting broad fields of stubble where pheasants would occasionally run out from under the hedgerows or a rabbit scamper across the road. You would note, too, the *abris* where the guns take cover during the shoot, when the "beaters" drive up the game. Great straw-stacks—*bonshommes de paille*, thatched with that deft nicety so characteristic of everything that the French farmer does—swell their comfortable rounded masses in colonies of six or eight against the setting sun, and presently you whirl through the pretty little town of Dammarie-les-Lys with its rose-embowered walls and ivy-clad gateposts, topped with vases of geraniums, only to find yourself once more out upon the broad plain which now sweeps downward toward a bend of the Seine.

A turn, and you enter a double avenue of lofty trees, a century or two old, and at its end see a high wrought-iron grille, one gate of which stands invit-

[18]

ingly open. Great stone retaining-walls, topped with ivy, extend limitless on either hand, while beyond the

The roadway describes a broad circle

grille a *tapis vert* stretches up to the château, gleaming cream-white among the clipped trees. The roadway describes a broad circle, and as you draw up under the glass marquise a tall footman runs down the carpeted steps to open the carriage door. A great wood fire greets you in the big drawing-room, whose windows cheerily face on the one hand the *tapis vert*, and on the other the broad expanses of the formal garden.

With what pleasure I recall the dinners in the hospitable dining-room; the evenings in the library with its dim array of aged volumes, its rare lithographs and *sanguines* by Boucher and his school glowing from the walls, while Holbein's portrait of Erasmus peeped from a corner as we sat about the glow of the great chimneypiece. And the alcove-beds upstairs with their faded chintz hangings, and the wall panellings of Trianon gray, enlivened with oval old-time paintings above the doors and mantelshelves! . . .

I

VAUX-LE-VICOMTE

BECAUSE of an extended residence in Fontainebleau, we had known these châteaux
for years. To us they were an old story.
Therefore, it was a constant source of surprise that
so few of our friends had even heard of them. In
fact, so little are they known that, instead of calling
them "Unfrequented Châteaux," I might almost
allude to them as unknown châteaux.

Of these châteaux about Melun, the most important
historically as well as artistically is Vaux-le-Vicomte.
While Louis XIV was still contenting himself with
the comparative luxury of his palaces at St. Germain
and Fontainebleau as they then existed, his chancellor, Fouquet, having carefully administered the affairs
of state largely to his own profit, determined to build
for himself a château that would eclipse anything his
royal master then possessed. He appointed Le Vau
his architect and Le Brun his artist-in-chief, and with

their help perfected a magnificent set of plans which cost sixteen million francs (an enormous sum for those days) to execute. When Le Vau's work was finished, Le Brun's began. He assembled at Vaux a veritable army of artisans and artists, and established himself there with his wife like a grand seigneur in an entire apartment on the first floor. A tapestry factory was established near by, at Maincy, where the elaborate hangings for the rooms and for the furniture were woven.

Le Nôtre, then at the beginning of his career, was next called in to plan the gardens, and they were his first great opportunity. Posterity has united in saying that he made the most of it. Hundreds of workmen changed this barren plain to a garden of enchantment, replete with every device that Le Nôtre's imagination bequeathed to the French school of landscape architects.

If we consider the amount of artistic effort expended in the construction and decoration of Vaux, in the architecture of its gardens and the making of its furnishings; if we stop to consider that Fouquet was a renowned collector of pictures, tapestries, statues, and rare prints; that his numerous portraits were graven in steel by twenty different engravers; that he collected coins and had numerous medals struck for himself—we can understand why he was called the Mæcenas of his day and why he merited the title.

But alas, his "fool's paradise," as it was called, proved his undoing!

When the château was finished he invited a great party, including Monsieur and his bride Henrietta of England, and a series of brilliant fêtes was inaugurated. But Fouquet's ambition stopped at nothing short of entertaining the King himself, and of showing his sovereign what the combined genius of such a galaxy of stars as Le Vau, Le Brun, Le Nôtre, and Vatel, his ever-to-be-remembered chef, could accomplish.

His ambition was finally gratified, for the King consented to come. Such extravagant fêtes as those then organised had never before been known. In the bosquets of the garden the guests found booths where dainties and rare perfumes and gifts were distributed; men whose propensity for gambling was well known, on awakening in the morning, found purses filled with gold upon their dressing-tables. The King was disgusted at this vulgar show of wealth, and jealous, too, if the truth be told, and while he exclaimed, "What foolish extravagance!" he noted, with all too evident irritation, Fouquet's device carved everywhere about the house: a squirrel running up a tree with the motto, "Quo non ascendam?"

The crowning glory of these fêtes was the performance by Molière and his troop of "Les Fâcheux," especially written for the occasion. It was given in the gardens by starlight. When the guests were seated, Molière appeared without make-up or costume, and apparently was dumfounded at seeing the King. He apologised for neither having his players with him nor a play to give. Just then there rose from the waters of a fountain near by a nymph in a shell. She gracefully stated that she had come from her home in the water's depths to behold the greatest monarch the world had ever seen. Started in this flattering key, this dainty conceit of a play went on to praise Louis at the expense of his courtiers, satirising them as *les fâcheux*—the bores—with their hobbies, their sycophancy, and foibles, and pleasing the King so extravagantly that he called up and congratulated the author, even suggesting a new character to be introduced—the *grand veneur* and his interminable stories of the hunt.

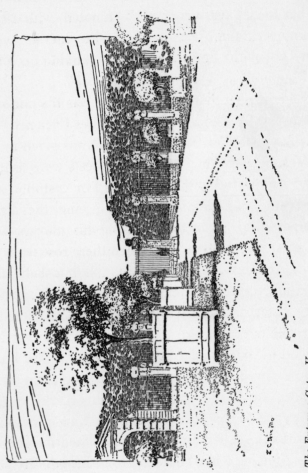

The Entrance Gates, Vaux

From that evening Molière was assured of the lasting favour of his King, and it marked the turning-point of his career from troubles and petty jealousies to fame and favour. La Fontaine, also one of Fouquet's pensioners, was among the spectators that evening, and his "*Songe de Vaux*" was written in memory of the occasion:

> Tout combattit à Vaux pour le plaisir du roi:
> La musique, les eaux, les lustres, les étoiles.

But the King amid his pleasures could not forget his jealousy, which reached its culmination when he heard that Fouquet had dared raise his eyes to the royal favourite, Mademoiselle de la Vallière. Eighteen days later the chancellor was arrested by the King's command and sent to prison for life.

Vaux passed into the hands of the Duc de Praslin, and still is often called by his name, Vaux-Praslin.

Unlike the châteaux that have become the property of the state to be made into museums, cold, uninhabited, and uninhabitable, Vaux retains to the utmost degree its pristine magnificence. Owned for many years by a man of great wealth, who had the respect of its traditions, it has lost none of its beauty.

Vaux-le-Vicomte

Its incomparable gardens stretch green in the sunlight, spreading their parterres and *boulingrins*, their fountains, statues, and great *pièces d'eau*, almost to the limits of the horizon. Armies of gardeners trim the pleached hedges, plant the elaborate borders, and remove every stray leaf from the gravel walks. It is the acme of formal French gardening.

The estate is separated from the county road by an imposing grille, with stone posts in the form of Hermes some thirty feet high. From this the main avenue, flanked by orange trees in tubs, slopes down between the *basse cour* and conservatories on one hand, and the carriage-houses and garages on the other, to the drawbridge. The whole château stands nobly raised on a great stone terrace reflecting itself on all sides in the waters of a broad moat. One mounts a wide rise of steps to the vast stone vestibule with its full equipment of liveried footmen in silk stockings and gold lace. From this vestibule the main *salons* lead off on either hand, with the beautiful paintings by Mignard and the two Le Bruns still glowing in alcove and lunette and in the coffers of the ceilings. The hangings, the furniture, wood-work, and panelling—much of it of the original period—are still fairly perfect in style, showing the faults, the pomposity, if you will, but the grave dignity of that courtly epoch of Le Grand Monarque.

Vaux-le-Vicomte from the Parterre

The great feature of the interior is a vast stone rotunda capped with the dome that forms so conspicuous a part of the garden façade. This *salle* serves as connecting link between the house and garden, for half of it is embedded in the château while the other half projects out of doors. Its circumference is equally divided by doors and windows, the doors leading into various adjoining drawing-rooms, the windows opening to the ground and affording beautiful vistas of the garden.

It is only on stepping from this rotunda out upon the terrace, from which a long flight of steps leads down, that the splendour and spread of Le Nôtre's garden architecture count for their full value. The planting is, of course, denser and richer than in Fouquet's day. The broad parterres, wider even than at Versailles, stretch away to the little river confined by rustic cascades, beyond which a broad upland rises, framed by a hemicycle of trees and decorated with an enormous gilded Farnese Hercules. The gardens are enriched with all the devices of Le Nôtre's art: fountains, great urns and vases, gilt statues, *rocailles*, and *treillages*. Some of the sunken gardens, notably that of the Bassin de la Couronne, still simulate the old *parterres de broderie*—designs carried out in clipped box-borders, whose compartments are filled with coloured stone and bits of glass. As a contrast to these vast sunlit spaces, the whole garden is surrounded by a *tonnelle* of clipped hornbeam, whose dense shade entices one in from the summer's sun and leads to shady boscages, cool seats, and niches where ghostly statues gleam in the shadows.

To many critics, though these gardens were Le Nôtre's first important work, they remain his greatest achievement.

II

LAGRANGE–BLÉNEAU

BEYOND Vaux-le-Vicomte, quite far out over the richly cultivated plains of the Brie, stands another great château that should be of particular interest to Americans, yet very few have either visited it or, indeed, even heard of its existence. I allude to Lagrange-Bléneau, the ancestral home of Lafayette, and, for the last thirty years of his life, his favorite place of residence. In all the five hundred years of its existence, Lagrange has never been bought or sold, it having passed to Lafayette by direct descent and thence on to its present owner, the Marquis de Lasteyrie, one of whose ancestors married Lafayette's daughter.

The nearest village, Courpalay, a mere group of houses, is about a mile or two away, Lagrange standing quite by itself out in the broad open fields that have always been its fruitful appanage.

As you leave the highway to take a by-road, you perceive to your left an avenue of trees at the end of which appears a dark mediæval gateway flanked by

massive round towers, fronted by a stone bridge that
has replaced the old drawbridge over the moat.

Château of Lagrange-Bléneau

This narrow gateway, just wide enough to admit
the passage of a modern motor-car, admits to a large,

stone-paved courtyard, surrounded on three sides by high buildings of fine solid masonry, while the fourth side, unenclosed, affords a view of the park with its ornamental trees and winding water courses.

In the doorway that opens in the far corner of this court, our host stood waiting to greet us—a man whose finely modelled head with its high aquiline nose, and whose lithe slender figure needed no externals of dress or manner to show that he is "de race."

With him, we mounted the broad stone staircase adorned with its numerous family portraits and busts: graceful eighteenth-century ladies of France and England (for the family has many English connections) in powdered wigs and paniers; Irish admirals, British generals in scarlet coats, diplomats, statesmen, all dominated and overshadowed, as it were, by Ary Sheffer's great full-length portrait of Lafayette painted toward the end of his life and almost a duplicate, if I remember correctly, of the one that hangs in the White House in Washington.

We then entered a circular drawing-room, arranged in one of the massive corner round-towers (of which there are five in the castle) with windows opening in all directions upon the park. The spaces between these windows were hung with either beautiful tapestries dating from the time of the Grand Monarque or with gleaming arrays of medallions, wax bas-reliefs and miniatures in jewelled frames of bygone members of the family.

In this room we sat until luncheon was announced, then descended to the dining-room whose rich walnut panels also framed superb Flemish tapestries of decorative design that completed a perfect ensemble of quiet dignity. During lunch we talked of many things and our host told, among other things, of how, without changing it in the least, he had endeavored to restore to the Château of Lagrange the physiognomy that it presented in the time of Lafayette and he has been most successful, I should say, as we found when we visited its various apartments. In the salons now stand the ancient commodes, the inlaid desks, the ormolu-mounted tables, the bergères and two precious chairs, signed by Jacob, that our host discovered not long ago hidden away in an attic and covered in the time of Louis Philippe with a coat of black enamel paint! The long corridors and hallways are hung with fine old engraved portraits, and with prints of naval combats and land battles. At the end of one of these corridors, upon which opens a series of guest-rooms, we crossed over the top of the feudal entrance-gate and a low door, thickly studded with great iron nails, swung open upon its heavy strap-hinges to our host's bedchamber which he had arranged in one of the massive towers that once defended the draw-bridge.

He told us that he had long hesitated between this room and the one that his illustrious ancestor had occupied during all the latter years of his life in another tower which he now proceeded to show us.

Retracing our steps down the long corridor, and mounting a narrow winding staircase, we entered that historic chamber, quiet, remote, in a part of the castle where no sound penetrates. It is a rather small room, decorated in the time and style of the Directorate. The head of the bed is in a sort of recess or alcove at each side of which a door admits to a closet, that cuts off the corner of the room. The panels of these doors are embellished with neo-classic ornaments in the Pompeian manner and the walls are hung with old prints. The room as a whole has a general air of seclusion and quiet comfort.

In a corner near the entrance, a narrow doorway,

penetrating the thick wall of another of the five towers to which I have alluded, admits one to Lafayette's library, certainly the most interesting room, historically, in the house. Being in a tower, it too is, of course, circular in form with a coved ceiling. All the wall spaces are occupied by bookcases, whose cornices are supported by tall, spindly columns, the shelves between glowing with the gilt tooling on the backs of old volumes bound in vellum and parchment. Upon a sort of frieze that runs between these bookcases and the ceiling, Lafayette had painted in grisaille bas-relief, profiles, simulating portrait coins, of many of his distinguished friends, among whom the American visitor notes with pleasure, just opposite the door, in the place of honor, as it were, likenesses of Washington, Jefferson, and Franklin.

It was at Lagrange that Lafayette lived in retreat and received all the distinguished friends and acquaintances who came to see him and do him homage during the latter years of his eventful life, and his strong personality still dominates and permeates the château just as his portrait dominates its staircase.

Later in the afternoon, we walked with our host through the park that has partially reverted to a state of nature, its long allées romantically overgrown with weeds and climbing vines, and as we walked, we discussed many subjects—comparative conditions of life in France and England, post-war problems, tendencies in art and literature—so that, when we departed late in the afternoon, we felt that we had spent a day in quite another epoch than our own hectic age, an epoch of quiet dignity and charm, when men took time for courtly manners, for graciousness and for the amenities of life.

III

COURANCES AND FLEURY-EN-BIÈRE

ON the Route d'Arbonne the beeches were beginning to yellow; the cool depths of the forest near Franchard held a refreshing suggestion of chill—refreshing after the long summer warmth—and farther on, in the open spaces, the pines cast long bluish shadows across the drying heather that October morning. But the drive through the forest was none the less perfect and our horses sniffed the brisk air with very evident pleasure.

And when we reached the confines of the woods, broad meadows lay before us and fields that lay fallow after the harvest. The air grew warmer and we passed through a little village, then turned out into the fields again until we came to small patches of woodland grown with youngish trees. A faint crepitation in the woods to the left—a sound that I knew very well—made Félix crack his whip and declare: "On chasse chez Monsieur le Marquis aujourd'hui."

Now and then a stray pheasant or a brace of partridges, escaping the beaters, would hum over our heads to the highlands at the right. But, except for a white flag or two on the edge of the wood, we saw never a sign of the guns whose volleys we could still hear from time to time.

Not long afterward another village came into sight and, leaving the carriage in front of the single little inn of which the town of Courances boasts, we wandered down the road to where the château lies, in a hollow far off the "beaten track," unsought, unknown to the tourist, unchronicled by Baedeker. We had driven there frequently before, but no matter how often seen, one can never fail to escape an *impression* at sight of the stately avenue that acts as approach.

This royal allée—a hundred yards in width and thrice as long, bordered on each side by wide canals, behind which rise double curtains of sycamores, centuries old, whose branches, trimmed high, droop down, down until they trail their leaves in the very water itself—leads from the entrance-gate to the square island upon which stands the château, its peaked roof and tall chimneys fittingly closing the vista.

Courances

It is quite a walk up this avenue and at its end you find yourself before a stone drawbridge. The château stands with its feet in the water, so to speak, mirroring itself in a broad moat to which groups of stately swans add life. The building, preceded by an immense stone forecourt, stands well back from the drawbridge and its four flanking pavilions. An exterior horeshoe staircase, evidently inspired by, and at all events reminiscent of, its neighbor at the Palace of Fontainebleau (in both cases a late excrescence and a disfigurement rather than an ornament), ascends to the main floor and entrance.

The château itself is a rarely perfect design of the time of Louis XIII, solid gray stone on its north or court side, brick and stone on its south or garden side, and the contrast between the sombre dignity of the one and the gay sunlit quality of the other is singularly effective.

Behind the château, the axis of the great avenue is again taken up by the central line of the beautiful gardens that are embellished with statues, fountains, *corbeilles,* and basins whose grotesque stone heads spout the water on to lower levels—all very formal in arrangement and quite in accord with the dignified old pile that they frame. These gardens are surrounded on all sides by dense woods, damp, moss-grown, and ivy-clad.

Courances from the Gardens

The interior of the château has been somewhat modernized, but the main floor retains all its old characteristics: rooms in sequence that occupy the entire width of the house without halls, their windows thus affording garden vistas to the south and views down the great allée to the north. They are furnished with taste and magnificence.

On the floor above, a corridor skirts the north side of the building, and opposite each of its windows a door opens into a bedroom, furnished in the classic French styles but with every modern comfort. Between these doors hang a series of rare Gobelin tapestries of exquisite workmanship, dating from the time of Louis XV, completely covering the wall spaces.

The present owners of Courances have the discernment and the means to keep it in a perfect state of preservation and to endow it with the pomp and circumstance that befit its stately appearance. They also owned until recently, another château, Fleury-en-Bière, not very far away, a fine old pile that had been allowed to fall into a state of decay until its present owner restored it within the last year or two.

Picking up our carriage again in the village, we drove off toward Fleury through an undulating landscape: hill slopes topped with woods and pastures, adjoining fields of grain and numerous clumps of coppice, ideal shelter for game with rich feeding-ground all about. The shooting that we had heard in the morning was again audible off to the right, and constantly grew nearer and nearer. Soon *rabatteurs* in white, carrying white flags, appeared coming toward us at a bend of the road, and presently a happy accident brought us into the very thick of the shoot.

It made a brave show indeed, stretching across the fields for a quarter-mile or so—seven "guns" only, spaced well apart, each followed by two men, one to reload and the other to pick up the game, while on the flank and behind, trudged quite a little army, nearly seventy in all. Bringing up the rear was a commodious covered wagon, carrying extra guns and laden with game. As the long line approached each thicket where the birds had taken cover, the "beaters" advanced, and pheasants and partridges whirled out in clouds to be saluted with volleys from the rapid-fire guns.

We may all have our ideas of how sportsmanlike a proceeding this is, and of how much real pleasure is derived from the mere killing of quantities of game; but in the bright sunshine of this October afternoon, it all made a very pretty picture and one long to be remembered.

As I have said, Fleury was our objective point, and

soon its long retaining wall of gray stone punctuated with angle watch-towers came into sight.

The estate stands in the open fields except for a tiny vassal town adjoining the château. This latter was built in the time of Henry IV, and still remains an exceptionally fine type of seigniorial residence of that period. A high stone wall, beautifully panelled in brick, with a fine gatehouse in the middle, screens from the road a vast forecourt bordered on each side by servants' quarters and stables panelled to match the wall, and at the back by the big château, reminding one of the old prints of the Cour du Cheval Blanc at Fontainebleau before Napoleon opened the court by replacing its outer wall with the present iron *grilles*.

The Château of Fleury is a simple but very dignified building of gray stone with round towers at its corners. At one end a wing projects, terminated by a very picturesque tower or group of towers, with high-pitched roofs, and the whole group of buildings is moated. Until recently, it had not been occupied in years and its interior had fallen into a state of woeful disrepair, though the original mantelpieces and much of the old wood-panelling still remained when

Corner of the Moat, Fleury

its present owner began its restoration. Though this restoration has been carried out with skill and taste, and its salons have a delightful eighteenth-century atmosphere, its real and unique feature, to my mind, is the great *basse cour,* or farmyard, whose like I do not remember to have seen except, perhaps, one on a hill beyond Larchant that belongs to the Chapter of Notre Dame.

This *basse cour* adjoins the main forecourt to the south and is surrounded on all sides by fine stone barns and wagon-houses, whose walls are divided into the same brick panels that form so characteristic a feature of Fleury's architecture. Great doors capable of swallowing entire hay-wains and topped with gables give access to the various granaries and hay-lofts. I can give no better idea of the extent of these buildings than to say that I have seen, during manœuvres, an entire battery of artillery quartered within this farmyard. Shepherds come back to it at eventide from the moist fields below the château with their flocks of sheep; at milking-time the cows wander in from rich pastures; turkeys strut triumphant in the sunshine and spread their tails; troops of fat geese and ducks hiss and cackle at the wayfarer; chickens

Fleury and its Church

pick in the manure piles, and sleek pigeons preen themselves upon the gables. It all takes one back to the days of one's childhood and the story of "Puss-in-Boots": "To whom do these broad acres belong?" "To the Marquis of Carabas." "To whom do these fat flocks belong?" "To the Marquis of Carabas."

. . . .

There are several other châteaux in the vicinity of Fontainebleau that are well worth a visit. There is Vaux-le-Penil, an imposing piece of eighteenth-century masonry, standing on a hill above the Seine near Melun; there is La Rochette, dating from a much earlier period, perched among its woods on the other side of the river; there is Fortoiseau, a happily preserved summer home of the time of Louis XVI; there is Graville, with its magnificent fireplaces of the time of Henry IV, with that King's portrait-bust in the central medallion; there is charming Bombon, set on its rectangular *terre-plein* surrounded on all sides by water and rendered historic by having been the headquarters of Marshal Foch during all the latter months of the Great War, and there are others still that need not be mentioned here.

MOTOR DRIVES

MOTOR DRIVES

I

TO PROVINS, SENS, AND NEMOURS

IT was a blustery June morning when we started from our home in Fontainebleau for this two days' jaunt. Big masses of billowy clouds flew ominously overhead only to give way to bright patches of sky and glistening sunlight, and after we had left the town and Valvins far behind, we enjoyed watching the great cloud shadows scurrying over the Bois de Valence, darkening the woods and racing along the roads as if to give chase to the motor car.

At the edge of the forest we turned off toward Montereau, which we soon discerned spreading its broad boulevards and embankments along the Seine and Yonne, which here come together. We stopped for a moment on the old stone bridge to evoke a picture of the assassination of Jean Sans Peur, Duke of Burgundy, who was induced to come out alone upon it, to a parley on the broad *terre-plein* in the middle, there to be murdered by the Dauphin's hirelings. Over in the great church of Notre Dame close by you can see his sword hanging in the nave up over the high altar.

Off again over the broad plains, the motor devoured mile after mile of long white road flanked by files of slender poplars, trembling and fluttering and bending their tall heads under the breath of the brisk west wind. How we pitched down the grades, only to puff up the next hill and rush across the plains beyond! I remember but three towns on the way: Salins and its old fortress castle; Montigny-Lencoup, with a giant cedar on the hill and its picturesque church turning its high buttressed apse toward the cross-roads, and Donnemarie, with another fine church and ancient gate and a gallery around its deserted graveyard.

Otherwise only the broad white road with its attendant trees—the expansive plains, vast and well cultivated—and then you come to a hill.

From its summit you look down upon a smiling town, set partly upon a hill top and partly at the junction of two valleys that surround this hill. This town, Provins, with its historic associations, its melancholy ruins, its bustling peasant life, the gaiety of

The broad white road and its attendant trees

its valley, its delicious cool ravines, choked with chestnut trees and terraced with hawthorn hedges and gardens, is to my mind one of the loveliest spots within easy access of Paris. Balzac (who knew his provinces well), in relating his sad story of Pierrette, which he lays here in Provins, does not hesitate to call it a terrestrial paradise—one of the most charming towns in France. And he goes further and declares that the Provinois love their town so well that they never leave it for longer than is absolutely necessary, and that the proverb, "Mourir au gîte"—made for rabbits and faithful people—seems, above all others, to have been intended for them.

Provins lies just about twenty miles from civilisation; that is to say, only twenty miles away trainloads of tourists go constantly thundering by in the big expresses to Switzerland. But only local trains stop at Longueville, from which station a little branch road runs to Provins. It is just for this reason—this comparative inaccessibility—that the town has retained its charm and character.

We drew up at the Golden Ball Inn. It was a Saturday and a market day, and the lower town bustled with life. Here at the hotel, as it happened, the Cercle Agricole of the region was having its annual or semi-annual banquet, and the place hummed with the good-natured chatter of a crowd of well-to-do farmers, red-faced, fat, and happy after their

The Rue Couverte, Provins

Pantagruelian luncheon. We were shown into a private dining-room which gave directly on the interior yard of the inn, which, of course, like all the hostelries of this town, is a relic of the old stage-coach days, for Provins in its day was an important stop on the great post road to the east of France, constantly furrowed by diligences, calashes, and coaches. The court, upon this occasion, was completely choked with every conceivable sort of vehicle, from heavy farm wagons and one-horse chaises to smart tilburys and motor cars.

We had a very good luncheon and after it set out for a stroll over the worn cobble-stones.

In the lower town we found the Church of Sainte Croix, with its exquisite flamboyant portal; the clock-tower of Notre-Dame du Val, resembling the famous old gateway at Amboise; and Saint Ayoul, a squat old church whose picturesque excrescences almost hide its antiquity. And it is an ancient pile, for in the priory attached to it Abelard once taught. We found, too, any number of quaint old houses and mills along the Durtain and Voulzie, the two rivers that drain the valleys referred to above.

But it is in the upper town that the chief interest of Provins lies. Like the Upper City at Carcassonne, it is quite deserted by modern life. But for that very reason, indeed, it has a melancholy charm that hushes the intruder, and one pokes silently and quite alone about its winding streets and along the old city walls with their ruined towers, their ivy-clad walls and moats choked with weeds and creepers.

The sensational monument is the donjon tower, La Tour de César, as it is called, a splendid specimen of feudal building. With its massive walls and high slate roofs, its cells and oubliettes, its huge reservoir to withstand a siege, it makes a stately relic indeed watching over its vassal town.

Saint Quiriace near by, though Provins's largest and most important church, possesses but few interesting details, for it has been sadly spoiled by restorations, and, worst of all, has been capped with an awful dome placed astride of the transept cross.

But we found compensation for its faults in the purity of style of the cross and well in the Place du Châtel; in the twelfth century Grange-aux-Dîmes (or granary for tithes), with its beautiful vaulted chambers; and in a rarely early and perfect house of the Romanesque period in the Rue du Palais.

Sens on a Fête Day

We did not get away from Provins till five o'clock. Once out of the town, we sped down the lovely valley of the Voulzie to its confluence with the Seine, crossing the latter river at Bray-sur-Seine, then climbing the hills beyond. An hour's drive over the uplands brought us to the brink of the valley of the Yonne, which river we struck at Pont-sur-Yonne, an ancient residence of the dukes of Nemours. Here a superb road leads along the river bank all the way to Sens, where we arrived by seven o'clock, just in time for dinner.

We found this town *en fête*, and spent the evening very pleasantly in wandering among the booths, in watching the crowds, and especially in assisting at a performance by strolling players at a portable theatre on the esplanade. What melodrama, what ranting, and what gesture—all of which the big, simple audience swallowed with bated breath!

The cathedral of Sens is, perhaps, notable for size rather than beauty, as we found on visiting it the next morning, but the interior is lofty, pure, and impressive, and the south portal or Portail d' Abraham, with its superb rose-window and rich traceries, especially called forth our enthusiasm. Adjoining the mother church is the Palais Synodal, a very pure piece of early Gothic deemed worthy of restoration by Viollet-le-Duc. We also found vestiges of an amphitheatre and temples in the very centre of the town, Sens having been a Gallic city of real importance even in Roman days. There is, too, a lofty fragment of the third century walls, pierced by a highly picturesque postern gate of a much later period out on one of the exterior boulevards, and scattered through the town one may discover many a half-timbered house ornamented with quaint wooden sculptures.

Our chauffeur met us in front of the cathedral, and by eleven o'clock whisked us across the Yonne, then up the high chalk cliffs that skirt its left bank. It was a very stiff climb indeed, even for a big motor, up a winding road, affording many fine views out over the valley and down upon the city, whose cathedral towers and Hôtel de Ville spire mounted high above its sea of blue-slate roofs. On attaining the summit, a broad upland plateau spread out before us, and we ate up the miles at a great rate.

A few people like ourselves enjoying the fine Sunday morning in motor cars, were about the only human beings we encountered.

Sens Cathedral from the Tapis Vert

Via Cheroy and Lorrèze, we attained Nemours in less than half an hour. We alighted for lunch at the Ecu-de-France, which Victor Hugo, an ardent ad-

The Château of Nemours

mirer of Nemours, cites in his "France et Belgique" as a typical *auberge* of rural France. And a rarely characteristic inn it is, preserving every feature of its olden days: its great kitchen, with its brave array of

coppers and brasses; its court-yard, stable-yard, and
well; its vast *salle* and small, quaintly furnished din-
ing-rooms, and its big-hearted proprietor and chef,
whose wife will always make you comfortable.

Standing before it and looking down at the church
below, who can repress a thought of little Ursule
Mirouet and her scheming relatives gathered round
its portal, as Balzac depicts them in his story so replete with descriptions of the pretty town and of the
country round about it?

We were joined here by my old friend M——, a
well-known landscape painter and a native of Nemours, and with him visited the château, once the
residence of the proud Guises, dukes of Nemours,
and inspected in detail its halls and tower-rooms and
its interesting little collections, winding up on the
top of its great donjon tower which overlooks the
pastoral valley of the Loing, so beloved by the artist
craft.

We were now nearing home again. An hour's ride
from Nemours brought us to Grez-sur-Loing, where
we stopped for tea and refreshments and to say
good-day to Madame Chevillon, whom we found,
as usual, in her kitchen preparing chickens for dinner.

Hers is a little hostelry that some years ago was a favourite resort of a rare group of men of whom

The Walls and Gate, Moret

Robert Louis Stevenson was the moving spirit. Its dining-room is still panelled in wood, each panel painted by an artist, many of them American and most of them since become famous. We took tea in the garden down by the glittering river beside the long stone bridge, painted times without number, that leads across to marshy lowlands, adorned with superb bouquets of cottonwood trees.

In the motor again we drove on to Marlotte, known to the world through Murger's "Vie de Bohême," and Montigny, both of these old haunts of ours, and then on to Moret, where we planned to dine at a little pleasure resort kept by Madame Chevillon's son. From its garden by the river we enjoyed the sunset: the reedy stream in the foreground, the fine stone bridge so often seen in Sisley's paintings, the city gates and walls, with the fretwork of the church, and the donjon towering against the evening sky. We thought of our friends over there in the town, taking their coffee in their quiet gardens by the river or close under the city wall, and the temptation was strong to pull the latch-strings that were always down. But we resisted, returning instead to Fontainebleau late in the evening through the depths of the forest.

II

TO ETAMPES, MAINTENON, AND CHARTRES

TWO days later we started for a second trip, this time turning our faces westward by the same Route d'Arbonne that we had taken in going to Courances. After four miles or so of forest land, we sped out onto the plain. And such a lovely picture it made that bright June morning, with its patches of wheat and barley alive with corn-flowers and poppies—field upon field of flaming combinations of yellow, red, and blue! The first large town on the road is Milly, where we stopped to have a look at its battlemented old castle near the inn where Henry IV once slept, and at the curious old open timber market-houses dating from the fifteenth century.

Bits of forest land, a village now and then, hills, quarries, and a river or two to cross, and we found ourselves coasting down into a broad valley with a long, white smiling town lying among groves of cottonwood trees and poplars planted with mathematical precision, like soldiers on parade in files and solid squares and phalanxes. This was Etampes. We

Old Mill near Etampes

arrived just in time to welcome a wedding procession to the embattled portal of the Church of Notre Dame. Its beautiful belfry is directly over the main door, and as we approached an old woman was ringing for the marriage service. She would pull down the bell with all her strength, and as it swung over it would hoist her off the ground and at least two or three feet into the air, when she would come down again with another great pull.

An imposing beadle warned us back as the country wedding party, awkward and red-faced in their unaccustomed finery, now alighted and filed into the church. We followed them in and watched the ceremony with interest, our amused curiosity centring upon the groom and his hunt for the ring in every one of his many pockets. He finally found it in his coat-tail in a box which he carefully opened. From this box he extracted the ring, closely wrapped in paper; then he unfolded the paper, placed the ring upon the bride's finger, refolded the paper, replaced it in the box and the box in his coat-tail pocket, and then, and not till then, did we breathe a sigh of relief.

Etampes has an old Hôtel de Ville, a dwelling of Louis XI's epoch, and two other remarkable houses —that of Diane de Poitiers, with a beautiful façade toward the court, and that of Anne de Pisseleu, Duchesse d'Etampes, both of the very best period of the early Renaissance, as, indeed, they should be, as the homes of two favourites of the lordly Francis, whose

Etampes, the Church

likeness we discovered cut in a medallion over one of Diana's doors.

We crossed the Juine, the little river that waters this fertile valley, and here had some difficulty in finding our road. The peasants wanted to send us to Rambouillet via Ablis, and we wished to go by way of Dourdan, to see its old castle built by Philip Augustus.

It is only about ten miles away, and when we once found the road it took us but little time to reach it. We felt well repaid for the trouble when we had viewed the vine-clad walls, the donjon, and nine lesser towers of this fortress, built by the very Philip who led the crusades with Cœur de Lion and was afterward victor at Bouvines.

After lunch we took the Route de Saint Arnoult, and, passing that town, entered the forest of Rambouillet, where the wire fences of game preserves appear on every hand. This forest is the special hunting ground of the President of France, and its *tirées* are stocked with quantities of pheasants, partridges, and hares, to be shot in veritable hecatombs by royal visitors and people of great distinction, guests of the Republic. Its northern confines

touch the Chevreuse district. How particularly
rich in monument and souvenir this Ile de France

The Castle of Philip Augustus, Dourdan

country is; yet how seldom is it properly explored
by tourists!

The Château of Rambouillet, though an extensive
pile, is of mediocre interest. To be sure, Francis I

[71]

died in the great round tower and Charles X signed his abdication here. But the palace has been modernised in sad official taste and has lost its character. Artistically, its only claim to distinction rests on a suite of rooms beautifully panelled in oak in the exquisite though florid style of Louis XV. A little room with rounded corners, called the boudoir of Marie Antoinette, is of special beauty. There are other souvenirs of this unfortunate queen in the beautiful gardens: a hermitage and *laiterie* built for her by her husband to recall her beloved Trianon, and a curious little bath-room, also bearing her name, entirely walled with Delft tiles.

The big main road from Paris to Chartres now took us on to Maintenon, which gave her title to Louis XIV's favourite, later his wife. The château here, now belonging to the Duc de Noailles, possesses many of the features of the better-known châteaux of Touraine and is a worthy rival to them. In style it is Louis XII and its high-pitched roofs and chimneys, its rich dormer-windows, its tourelles and finials, form a rarely picturesque sky line. Its north front of cold gray stone facing the entrance court is dignified and formal, but the south façade is a perfect riot of arcades, galleries, and balconies surmounted by towers, round, square, and octagonal. It faces upon a broad parterre whose parapets are decorated with pots of flowers, and the whole

Château of Maintenon

château stands encircled by wide canals fed by water from the Eure. Louis XIV evolved a scheme which was never completed, to bring this water to his gardens at Versailles, and the gigantic aqueduct that he began and on which he employed thirty thousand men for four years, its arches rivalling in size the aqueducts of the Campagna, still remains at the lower end of the Château Park to attest his extravagance.

The interior of the château can sometimes be visited. Madame de Maintenon's room preserves much

The great plains of the Beauce

of its old-time character, and Rigaud's portrait of her still hangs in the long gallery among portraits of the long line of ancestors of the Noailles family.

The road from Maintenon to Chartres traverses the great plains of the Beauce, one of the richest agricultural districts of central France, a region whose fields are extensive enough to encourage the use of the most improved farming machinery. In huge

Chartres Cathedral

courts, teeming with prosperity, you catch glimpses as you pass of big white oxen yoked in pairs by iron chains; of long-eared pink hogs rooting by ponds alive with ducks; of hens leading their chicks

Château de Bénéhart

to scratch in vast manure piles and of herds of sheep under the watchful care of collie and shepherd.

Soon to the left two points appear upon the horizon and become brighter and brighter, loftier and loftier; then the body of a church looms up like the hull after the masts of a ship at sea and you realise that you are approaching Chartres.

Chartres Cathedral, as is very well known, is perhaps the finest flower of the Gothic spirit in church architecture. Of pure and noble proportions, more harmonious and consistent in design than most of the churches of its period, it rises like a huge, solid rock, ribbed and scarred by man and by the elements, but strangely fresh and living, its soaring vaults held aloft by mighty buttresses, its spires complete, its windows still glowing with their jewelled glass, its portals still peopled with their rigid arrays of saints and angels.

To attempt even a brief description of its manifold beauties, would require a better pen than mine and many more pages than I feel that I have at my disposal here, so I shall not try to explain to the reader why the stern and simple south tower is considered better than its richer and more flamboyant neighbor; why the jesse windows of its chancel aisles rank with the finest stained glass in the world, nor why the dignity and nobility of the Gothic statues that adorn the niches of its various portals are considered the chef-d'œuvres of their kind.

The next morning (it being a Sunday) we attended mass in this grand Cathedral and never have

I heard the organ's notes swell more harmoniously in its mighty vaults nor seen it look more glorious than it did that Sunday morning, with great beams of golden light striking aslant from the clerestory windows down upon the congregation massed within the nave, and focussed, as it were, upon the white surpliced figure of the prebendary preaching from the pulpit.

Nor must I forget to say a word for the picturesque streets of Chartres (which most tourists neglect), especially those to the south of the Cathedral that lead down to the River Eure at the bottom of the hill, whose slow-moving waters are bordered by innumerable *lavoirs* and tanneries and spanned by little bridges defended by such feudal gateways as the Porte Guillaume, sketched a thousand times and beloved alike by painters and etchers.

III

TO THE VALLEY OF THE LOIRE

BEFORE noon, next day, we were speeding along again over the broad flat fields of the Beauce, extending almost level to a far horizon and with scarcely a sign of life. We lunched by the roadside under a clump of apple-trees on delicious game patties (a specialty of Chartres) stored away before our departure, and some excellent Chablis perfectly iced for the occasion in thermos bottles.

Another twenty miles or so and we gained Châteaudun, where we tarried long enough to see its grand old castle perched upon an abutting crag high above the River Loir. It is a ruinous old pile, once the residence of Dunois, the celebrated Bastard of Orleans, and it looks, I imagine, much as Langeais must have looked fifty years ago before its restoration. One wanders now quite at will up its spiral staircases and into its vast bare halls with stone stags couchant on the mantel-shelves, and out on narrow terraces overhanging, giddily, the deep rift of the valley below.

As we left Châteaudun, we ran into one of those sudden summer storms that are so frequent in France. All at once the clouds gathered ominously, the distances turned gray and foggy, then the nearer planes grew dim and wet, and the road glittered and became slippery under our tires as we bowled along in heavy showers of rain. It looked as if we were in for a real rainy day but presently, as quickly as it had disappeared, the sun began to peep forth again and tinged every object—trees, grass, and stones, with a brilliant golden light shadowed sharply with blue.

As we approached Patay, the sun had really triumphed once more and the larks, full-throated, were mounting aloft in full song. It was at Patay, some one remembered, that Dunois and Joan of Arc defeated the English forces and so we knew that we were approaching Orleans.

A windmill beating the air with its old creaking sails; families of raggle-taggle gypsies making or mending baskets by the roadside; bits of woodland road; stacks of barley drying in the stubble; children crowning each other with wreaths of leaves and flowers, like nymphs and youthful fauns—these were the sights along the road; then suburbs and *lotissements,* and the long dingy streets of the quarter of St. Loup. Presently we were entering Orleans itself and were stopping in the little square to the south of the Cathedral to admire its stalwart buttresses, the magnificent rose window of its transept and the pinnacles and crocketed spires cutting their sharp silhouettes against the sky. We preferred indeed this view of the Cathedral to its west front, a strange debased sort of Gothic façade erected under Louis XV—unusual, if you will, and possessing a certain merit undoubtedly, but all too reminiscent of those antiquated clocks, made of gilt-bronze, that used to grace the centre of mid-Victorian mantelpieces.

About the Cathedral are several points of interest. We greatly admired the little lead fountain—a boy with a swan supported by youthful tritons—that embellishes the square in front of the Cathedral and of the same period as its façade but a work of art in perfect consonance with the ideals of the eighteenth century. Then too one should visit the old Hôtel de Ville but a few steps away. Once a royal residence, it was in this building that Francis II died in the arms of Mary Stuart. It has been frequently re-modelled but still contains some very interesting rooms, chiefly of the sixteenth century. Behind it is a romantic little garden, deeply shaded by chestnut trees, and adorned by a lovely late-Gothic portico transported from the abbey of St. Jacques that used to stand where the ugly covered market now shelters its teeming throngs. There is quite a good Museum of Fine Arts and a Musée Jeanne d'Arc containing many interesting souvenirs of the Maid of Orleans, whose story is so closely linked with this ancient city by the Loire.

We left Orleans by the streets that lead down by the river—the broad turbulent, swift-flowing stream, whose banks we were now to follow and which is here spanned by a long nine-arched bridge, that, with its picturesque old houses, suggests a dry, meticulous etching by Meryon. The road follows the river for awhile, then turns up a hill and passes the Auberge de la Montespan, one of those recently established hostelleries to which I have alluded, established in a fine old château overlooking the Loire.

Soon we were passing through Meung-sur-Loire, replete with historic associations, often mentioned in the tales of the valley and the birthplace of Jean de Meung, known to all lovers of Chaucer's "Romance of the Rose." Three miles away, to the north, Louis XI lies buried in the little village church of Cléry, he having always worn in his cap a leaden image of Our Lady of Cléry, his patroness.

But a short distance beyond Meung, Beaugency comes into sight, its silhouette punctuated by the massive bulk of its great donjon tower and by the delicate spires of its principal church. Most tourists pass it by, little suspecting from its broad main thoroughfare that, down in the crooked streets to the left, lie some notable remains of mediæval architecture, grouped, for the most part, around a small and peaceful *place* at the foot of the donjon tower. This square is still entered by its old fortified gateway and is further adorned by a romanesque church of ancient and primitive design whose organ happened to be playing the morning of our visit, its sweet and plaintive notes greatly aiding the romance of the moment as I stood looking up at the old walls of the keep, whose little fenesters, like eyes, had witnessed many a siege and hard-fought battle, even those waged by Joan of Arc herself.

The Gardens, Château de Menars

From Beaugency the road stretches straight and almost level, through vineyards on either hand and pleasant-looking farmhouses that already begin to suggest the comfort and opulence of Touraine, to Blois.

But, as this road tempts you to speed along, do not speed too fast, but about five miles before you reach your destination, watch out for the little town of Menars. Slowing down as you pass through it, you will catch a glimpse, to the left, of a majestic, emblasoned grill, set in a great frame of overarching trees, through which appears a superb château whose tawny-colored walls and high-pitched roofs evoke the Grand Siécle.

Built by Guillaume Charron, father-in-law of the great Colbert, the Château of Menars was afterward owned and greatly embellished by Madame de Pompadour and her brother, the Marquis de Marigny. To the latter is credited the reconstruction of the château itself, and to her the arrangement of the beautiful gardens that descend in terraces toward the Loire. A lovely circular *temple d'amour,* a few good busts of Roman emperors, some fine stone vases and balustrades are all that remain of the innumerable objects of art that once were the pride of these gardens but which were destroyed during the Revolution. There is still enough, however, to evoke a very complete picture of one of those handsome, seigneurial gardens à la Française, well-ordered, carefully designed, that have been so aptly denominated "Jardins de l'Intelligence."

A few miles more and we enter Blois.

BY-WAYS IN TOURAINE

BY-WAYS IN TOURAINE

I

SOME FEUDAL CASTLES

MOST visitors to Blois content themselves with a visit to the celebrated Château, and that of course is quite as it should be, but this visit, in my opinion, should certainly be supplemented by a walk through the narrow, twisting streets of the old town, up to the Cathedral of St. Louis, not so much, however, to see this old bastard Gothic edifice nor Gabriel's handsome Bishop's Palace that stands behind it, as to step out upon the broad terrace beyond, shaded by its quadruple rows of ancient chestnut-trees, and there, near Anna Hyatt's spirited statue of Joan of Arc, to look out over the vast prospect that unfolds itself before you, your first real glimpse of Touraine.

The terrace below is carpeted with the beflowered parterres of the Bishop's garden, laid out in patterns like a Persian rug, while lower still the pink chimneys and high-pitched gables of the town interlock into the most intricate designs. Beyond these, roll the murky waters of the Loire with, upon the opposite bank, broad, rich plains, thickly interspersed with the dark masses of the forest lands that surround Chambord and Cheverny.

Toward evening, when the view is best, the sun gilds all this with a ruddy glaze, spreading its golden splendor even over the great thunder-heads that peer above the horizon far off toward Bourges.

This then should be the tourist's first view of Old Touraine, a land of beauty and romance that is fairly saturated with history. No other river that I can call to mind, except, perhaps, the Rhine, has so many stories to tell as the Loire. The stories of the Rhine are mostly legends, however, or, at best, concern historic personages of secondary importance, while the stories of the Loire form a sequence of the greatest names in French history.

Upon its shores, before Tours, Charles Martel beat back the Saracens; Richard the Lion-Heart and England's Plantagenets, born Counts of Anjou, beseiged its castles; Joan of Arc walked its roads and

fought here for her youthful King; the crafty Louis
XI imprisoned his enemies in its dungeons; the
lordly Francis gathered here his artists and his mis-
tresses. The intrigues of Catherine de Medicis, the
assassination of the Duc de Guise, the Huguenot
plots and counterplots all took place in its palaces,
and to all the Kings of France, until Louis XIV built
Versailles, Touraine remained the land of their pre-
dilection.

And its place in the history of art and letters is no
less distinguished. It was the cradle of the French
Renaissance that has so profoundly affected all the
modern forms of architecture. Jean Fouquet, the
"father of French painting," was born in Touraine;
Leonardo da Vinci, as legend has it, died in the arms
of Francis I in the old manor-house of Clos Lucé
near Amboise; while, in the domain of literature the
list is even longer and more illustrious. Rabelais
was born at Chinon; Balzac near Tours. Walter
Scott's "Quentin Durward," the scenes of many of
Balzac's stories and of most of his "Contes Drola-
tiques," Dumas's "Three Musketeers" and "Vicomte
de Bragelonne," Hugo's romances, de Vigny's "Cinq
Mars," all had their setting in this lovely land of

Touraine whose charm has fired the imagination of every artist and writer who has known it.

It is not my purpose, in this chapter, to take the reader to the well-known Châteaux of Touraine, glorious as their story is in history and in art, but rather to introduce to the more leisurely traveler a group of old feudal castles that lie within easy reach of Tours and near the more famous Renaissance châteaux, but which are quite unknown, I think, to the average tourist.

These castles, for the most part, formed links in the chain of fortresses that stretched along the river from Amboise to Saumur, built by the powerful Counts of Blois or the no less potent Counts of Anjou to protect their respective fiefs. The wars that these feudal lords and their retainers waged against each other make up most of the history of the French middle ages.

The first castle that we shall visit, however, is not one of these feudal strongholds but a complete and romantic picture of a lordly residence of the fifteenth century. It lies buried down beyond Chambord among the dense woods and marshes of the Sologne, a country famous alike for its game and its tales of marauding poachers and here, not far from the village of Lassay, you will find the ancient Château du Moulin, not, however, the Castle of the Mill, as its name might imply, but named for the family that built it. For four hundred years it has remained in the possession of this same family and, though their name is no longer du Molin (old spelling), it has been directly transmitted from one generation to another.

On every side, it still bathes its feet in the broad and placid waters of its moat, there being but one means of direct access to it: a narrow bridge (once a drawbridge) that leads to a superb fortified gate, surmounted by a machicolated parapet and flanked by the two tall towers that used to defend its bridge. To the left hand tower is attached the main body of the château, which terminates, at its other end, in another massive cylindrical tower, crenelated and capped to-day with its pointed roof *en poivrière*. Near to the main château, but entirely separated from it, rises a second building, very tall and elegant in proportion, almost square, but prolonged at one corner by a fine round tower and on another by the apse of a small chapel, the two groups of buildings forming a highly picturesque ensemble.

The walls and corner towers that once defended the castle and were all mirrored in the broad moat, have been razed to the height of the terre-plain on which the château is built, and now form only a low parapet around the castle. But even without them, or, perhaps, because they have disappeared and a better view of the tall principal buildings is thus disclosed, the whole composition, no matter from which angle it is viewed, still forms a rarely perfect picture of a feudal castle with its pale pink walls, often diapered with patterns in brick (for, unlike most of the châteaux of Touraine, Le Moulin is built of brick) and its high slate roofs, with their battlements and crocketed dormer windows, reflected in the still waters about them.

Its present owner, who inherited the castle in a rather dilapidated condition, has made careful restorations and, without losing any of its charm and picturesqueness, has been able to adapt it to the needs of a comfortable modern residence.

When you leave Blois for Tours, you will plan to stop, of course, at Chaumont, with its memories of Catherine de Medicis and her sinister astrologer, and at Amboise, also, perched high upon the massive

Château du Moulin

round towers that dominate the river and serve as its foundations. Instead of continuing directly on, however, I would suggest a detour over the hills to the valley of the Cher.

Ascending the narrow valley to the south of Amboise, you pass Clos Lucé, where Leonardo once lived and in which, as I have already stated, he died. Hence, a beautiful retrospect of Amboise is disclosed, the town lying snug and close to the waters of the Loire and dominated by its castle, massive as a cliff, rising abruptly above it, the sky-line perforated by the delicate foliations of the dormer windows and the traceries of its slender chapel spire.

The road now leads up and down through little forests of oaks and beeches, interspersed with dainty birches and cut by by-paths that beckon an almost irresistible temptation to wander down to the peep of blue sky at the end. A teamster's call, a dog's bark are the only sounds that break the stillness. How cool the shade; how fresh and pungent the odor of ferns and the rich, warm earth!

A succession of gently rolling slopes and then the valley of the Cher comes into view, stretching out in richly cultivated fields off to the far horizon. A long coast, a turn to the left and you are before the iron grills and the dark avenue of lindens, guarded by couchant sphinxes, that leads to the Château of Che-

Chissay

nonceaux—that jewel-box, given to Diane by her royal lover, so light, so airy, so smiling, so beautifully bestriding the river, that its charms have been sung and its story told times without number.

If, when you leave Chenonceaux, you turn eastward and follow the river valley upon the highway that eventually leads to Bourges, you will catch a glimpse to the left, if you watch out, of the beautiful Château of Chissay. From the gate, it makes a perfect composition, resembling in many ways one of the fine old English castles. A road, turning through wide, green lawns, backed by clipped hedges and shaded by noble cedars and oak-trees, conducts to a steep flight of steps that lead, with many turnings, in zigzags, up to the château, whose white façade and high-pitched roofs, strengthened at the corner by a huge round tower, gleam brilliantly against the dark foliage that clothes the hill behind it. Lofty trees in the foreground cast shadows over broad stone terraces and set the whole picture back as in a frame.

A mile or two beyond Chissay, you enter a village street and the great square keep and the imposing ruined towers of Montrichard appear, capping a steep hill around the base of which the village clusters. Montrichard was originally constructed by the Black Falcon, Foulques Nerra, that redoubtable builder of Angevin strongholds whose name appears so often in the history of these feudal castles of Touraine. From him it passed into the possession of his descendants, the English Kings, and it undoubtedly owes its name, Richard's Mount, to the fact that its mighty walls were strengthened and finished by Richard Cœur de Lion.

From Montrichard let us turn southward for ten miles or so to visit another of Foulques Nerra's citadels, Montresor. In its enormous foundation walls in which are engaged the ruins of mighty round towers, one again recognizes the handiwork of the Black Falcon. After him, like its neighbor, Montrichard, Montresor belonged to the Henrys of England, to Philip Augustus and then to Jean de Bueil, Grand Arbalétrier of France, who died on the field of Agincourt.

Of the original castle little remains except the gigantic foundation walls to which I have alluded. But upon them, at the end of the fifteenth century, as upon a giant pedestal, the present château was erected, a rectangular building flanked with towers, and, with its steep roofs cut by delicate dormers, resembling the wing of Louis XII at Loches. Though but a fragment of the magnificent château built here by Imbert de Batarnay, in its present state Montresor makes a charming place of residence, its owner, the Count Branicki, having furnished it with taste and discrimination.

An aged servitor led us through its rooms and showed us, among other things, the jewels and gold plate that once belonged to the Kings of Poland, of whom, if I remember rightly, the Count is a direct descendant. Before leaving I advise the visitor to cross the little stream, an affluent of the Indre, that flows at the bottom of the hill, and look back at the castle, perched high upon the great terrace walls, grim and forbidding. It and its outhouses and its shadowy park, and the houses of the village that cluster round the base of the walls, reflected in the slow-moving waters, upon whose quiet surface float water-lilies, reeds and other aquatic plants, make an extremely pretty picture whose particular attraction lies in the contrast of these grim and formidable ruins with a castle and a landscape so smiling and so peaceful.

The road to Tours leads through the valley of the Indre via Loches, which I describe in the next chapter, to Montbazon, the last of the great Angevin citadels that defended the south bank of the Loire. All that remains of it is a vast square donjon tower, ivy-grown and heavily buttressed and now capped with a colossal bronze statue of the Virgin—a striking landmark for miles around.

Here (to change our fare for a moment) I should recommend a little excursion up the valley of the Indre as far as the village of Saché, not so much, however, to see its dilapidated château, as to visit one of the rooms within it—a chamber that will thrill the heart of any true lover of Balzac. In the old Gothic castle, dwelt two friends of his, the de Margonnes. After one of those periods of stress and torment that were forever besetting his eventful life, Balzac craved their hospitality for a stay of some duration and, in the peace and solitude of this romantic valley, wrote some of the most brilliant pages of his immortal "Comédie Humaine." Here he conceived "Le Lys dans la Vallée," picturing its chaste heroine living in a charming old farm that he discovered opposite Pont-du-Ruan, and after her life of purity and self-sacrifice (founded upon the life of his life-long friend, Madame de Berny), he imagined her death and her burial in the little cemetery, filled with roses and honeysuckle, and suspended like a flower garden above the road opposite the château gate, in the very shadow of the venerable church of Saché.

And here too, with his abnormal double-tracked mind, he conceived and wrote the final tragic pages of "Père Goriot." And the room in which he wrote them exists to-day quite as when he used it.

Up a spiral staircase and shut off from all the rest of the house by double sound-proof doors, this small, gray, panelled room gave him just the seclusion that he needed. The alcove-bed with its rose-colored coverlet of toile de Jouy, his lamp that kept company with his all-night vigils, his paper-cutter, his arm-chair —all are there. And the views from the window with the tall dark firs and pines and the glimpses of the peaceful valley beyond, are quite as he knew them. So it takes but little effort of the imagination to see this giant of the mind working here feverishly day and night for whole days, with no food but black coffee and almost no sleep, until the last page of "Père Goriot" lay upon the table with its last phrase written, followed by the date: Saché, September, 1834.

.   .   .   .

It is quite natural that, along the northern bank of the Loire, there should also remain a number of medieval castles. Some of them, due to continued wars as well as the ravages of time, are no more than

Luynes still perches proudly

crumbling ruins; other still stand haughtily bristling with all their loopholed towers intact.

Of proud Plessis-les-Tours, just outside of the

[102]

city of Tours, once the favorite residence of Louis XI and the castle in which he died, only a rather commonplace manor-house. freely restored during the last century, remains.

But, a little farther down the river, the grand old Château de Luynes still perches proudly upon a commanding hill-top above its vassal town, like an eagle upon a feudal nest, its many towers sturdily protecting the short curtain walls that separate them and the whole composition crowned with tight-fitting slate roofs that glisten bravely in the sun. Though now unoccupied, it still belongs to the Duc de Luynes.

Beyond it, crowning another rocky eminence, the two massive round towers of Cinq Mars, shorn of their tops, recall to any lover of French literature, the tragic and celebrated story of Alfred de Vigny's, "Cinq Mars." For, in this now crumbling ruin, inhabited only by a retired army officer and his wife, was born that romantic figure, that handsome young man, Henri Coëffier, who went to court, became a Captain in the Guards and a favorite of his King, Louis XIII, who made him Grand Ecuyer de France. But, unfortunately for him, through his inordinate ambition, when but twenty-two years of age, he crossed the path of Richelieu, incurred his enmity, was arrested, accused of treason (that vague and terrible crime), and ordered decapitated, while this, his castle, according to the custom of the time, suffering the same fate as its master, was decapitated also and razed "à hauteur d'infâmie."

A few miles farther down the river, we enter the town of Langeais, one of the oldest in Touraine, and find, standing proudly at the end of the village street, the celebrated château that still bristles with all its crenelated towers and battlemented walls intact, presenting today perhaps the most complete picture extant of a French feudal castle. Thanks to the intelligent restorations of its last owner (who has now presented it and all of its collections to the Institute of France) and to his rare discrimination in selecting the authentic Gothic furniture and marvellous mille-fleurs tapestries that decorate its many rooms, its interior forms as perfect a picture of the life of the fifteenth century as its exterior, so that the Château of Langeais may well serve the traveler as a precious document upon which to construct the completed picture of each of the crumbling castles that he has now visited.

Another magnificent château of this same period still in an excellent state of preservation, is Ussé, which lies a little farther down the river but upon the opposite bank. What a glorious picture it presents as you see it from the entrance-gate! Broad terraces, decorated with parterres à la Française designed by Vauban (whose daughter married one of its erstwhile chatelains, Louis Bernin de Valentiné) serve as a gay setting for the château, whose exterior walls retain all the severity of the feudal Gothic castle, with machicolated ramparts, defended by a great array of towers of different shapes and sizes, while the façades of the interior court are smiling and gay, enlivened with delicately carved windows, with sculptured balconies, with fretted buttresses and crocketed pinnacles. Out in the garden stands an exquisite little chapel, reminiscent of the one at Amboise, that contains some fine bas-reliefs and some beautiful sixteenth-century glass.

From Ussé, we may easily continue our visits to these medieval châteaux by proceeding on to two that are indeed much better known: Chinon and Loches.

II

CHINON AND LOCHES

WE climbed the steep stairs to the château of Chinon on a bright sunny morning, mounting between walls of almost Oriental brilliance with only a peep of the deep blue sky above our heads. As we looked up, two peasant women in white caps nodded a greeting from the parapet above and we had a suspicion of red chimney-pots high above them.

A broad walk, shaded by trees, led us past the remains of the oldest part of the castle, and soon we had crossed the moat and entered the gate. Crumbling ruins and massive towers with grass-grown battlements surrounded us on every side. The extent of this grim old fortress-castle is tremendous, but decay has set its finger on the place and all that remains are caved-in passages, fragments of fireplaces, and tottering window-frames.

Chinon from the Market-place

IN TOURAINE

Memories of Jeanne d'Arc cling about the place, for here she came to wake the idle king from his life of ease, and, after weeks of prayer, from here she set forth to lead the French army to victory. Despite time's devastation, the tower wherein she lived while

The Castle, Chinon

at Chinon is still to be seen, and a large fragment of the room in which her first interview with the king took place.

But the great attraction of the giant walls is a walk along the parapet and a glance at the glorious panorama which lies at one's feet. The peaceful valley of the Vienne stretches as far as the eye can see. The distant hills are spotted with villages and châteaux;

the well-tilled fields, with their ripening crops, stretch from the banks of the river which winds like a broad silver band from horizon to horizon, spanned just beneath by a great stone bridge.

At our feet, so close that we can look down the chimney-pots, nestles the old Gothic city. Its four churches raise their backs above the neighbouring houses, but all else is a compact mass of blue slate roofs, high pitched, with dormer-windows and innumerable chimney-pots. Little pointed tourelles cling to the corners and far below we catch a hint of stone-paved streets. These few zigzag streets wind along the river more or less parallel to its course, affording at every turn new glimpses of fascinating gables, Gothic windows with their crumbling tracery, and houses whose huge timbers have withstood the wear of centuries, but whose paneless windows are now but the resting-place of countless spiders. Few, however, of these houses have been abandoned, and in nearly all of them the windows are adorned with rows of potted geraniums, brilliantly lighting up the cold gray stone.

Women in white caps lead little donkey-carts through these quaint old lanes or peddle fruits and

An Old Street, Chinon

vegetables in baskets of queer design, gossiping with
their customers on the way and vending news as well
as their wares. Thursday is market-day, and the
town wakes to a state of unwonted activity. From
the early morning hours, peasants begin to arrive at
the Place de l'Hôtel de Ville, and there set up their
booths and awnings. Soon huge pyramids of arti-
chokes arise, and stands of potted plants; fruits, cheap
calicoes, shoes, hardware, ribbons, and laces and all
conceivable kinds of fancy articles are arranged in en-
ticing array. By eleven o'clock the babel of tongues
becomes alarming! Women in strange coifs, men in
blue blouses and *casquettes*, haggle and quarrel over
their purchases. Two shepherds with pipes add a
most unearthly screeching, and are rewarded with
numerous sous. One hardware dealer, who attracts
attention to his wares by blowing a bugle, is outdone
by a rival who has a drum with a patent crank attach-
ment to keep it beating all the time. In the afternoon the old women meet at the goose market and
around the venders of butter and eggs. Then is the
time to see the wonderful collection of coifs. Each of
the surrounding villages has its own particular head-
dress. Many are made of the finest lace and some are

Loches

of great size. One of the most elaborate has been
given up because recent generations have gradually
lost the art of laundering it, and now only a few
women will take the trouble to wear it.

Toward five o'clock the crowd begins to diminish.
By dark the streets become deserted; an occasional
lantern projecting from a house-corner sheds its dim
light. Alleys lead to unknown mysteries of darkness.
Voices issue from the dwellings, and the sweet scent
of honeysuckle is borne over the high street walls.
Occasional glimpses are caught of dimly lighted interiors, where old women sit knitting or eating their
meagre *pot-au-feu*, or of a family gathered round the
evening meal in such a light as Gerard Douw so
loved to paint. By ten o'clock the old town slumbers,
and as we go to rest the only sound that greets our
ears is the splash of the fountain in the square below
our window.

DISTINCTLY sombre memories hang over the old
town of Loches. Though situated in a wide and fertile valley, watered by the sparkling waters of the Indre, it rises like a gaunt fortress on the crest of its hill,
the roof-tops piling up to its broad crown of walls, hold-

ing, within their strong embrace, the lofty towers of
its château, its abbey church, and the tremendous
stone mass of its donjon, about whose walls great
flocks of crows continually soar, filling the air with
their strident cries. This grim fortress-prison hid the
crimes of Louis XI, and here were kept all personal

Rises like a fortress

enemies of the crown accused of that broad crime of
"treason." What tales its echoing walls could tell!
What memories cling about its black cells and oubliettes! Here, for nine years, Ludovico Sforza was confined in a cell whose walls are covered with rude frescoes which his hand traced—crude likenesses of himself with casque on head, and a small sun-dial, by
whose aid he could count the waning hours of the

lonely days as the single ray of sunlight filtered through his solitary window. Below his cell is another bearing marks still more touching. In it were confined three bishops accused of treason to the state. On the wall, opposite the slit of a window which gave them their only light, they cut a rough crucifix in the stone. On one side of it, a small recess was made for their Bible, and on the other a hollow, in which the holy water was kept. At this primitive altar they celebrated their mass during two years. They climbed, by means of several dents in the stone, to the window-slit to see the one atom of green hill-top which was their only glimpse of dear mother earth. Adjoining is a still darker chamber without a ray of light (hollowed in the solid rock of the hillside), which, with its dreadful oubliette in the corner, is a fearful reminder of the "Pit and the Pendulum." It takes but little imagination to picture the life in this awful prison, with Cardinal de la Balue swinging in his iron cage, and the Duc d'Alençon with a great chain riveted round his neck, dragging himself before his guards. And, strange fate, the torture-chamber, whose rack is still in place, is now filled with cots, a resting-place for homeless tramps.

The Porte Picoys and Hôtel de Ville, Loches

This donjon, with its surrounding towers and fortifications, occupies one end of the walled space which constituted the upper city, to which access was only gained by means of a massive battlemented gateway with drawbridge and moat. The other end of the upper city was occupied by the royal château, a picturesque pile of buildings with numerous *pignons* and turrets.

Agnes Sorel, "*La Dame de Beauté*," and Charles VII lived and loved here, and she was buried in the abbey church. In the château we see her tombstone surmounted by a recumbent figure with angels watching over her head and with her little feet resting in the fleece of two young lambs. Hers seems the only sweet and peaceful figure in these grim surroundings, though Nature wears a smiling face as one views her from the broad parterres where Agnes must have walked with her royal lover.

Between the château and the donjon rises the distinctive feature of Loches, the abbey church of Saint Ours; "a church," says Viollet-le-Duc, "unique in the world—a monument of a savage and a strange beauty." It was the nucleus about which the city grew, its foundation having been laid as far back as the fifth century, but the present church was built some six hundred years later. It is preceded by a deep porch, which leads to the main entrance, remarkable for its magnificent archivolt, sculptured with queer figures of saints and allegorical animals and emblems. The first bay of the nave forms an interior vestibule and is surmounted by a massive tower, whose upper story is octagonal in form with a stone pyramidal steeple. The nave, properly speaking, has but two square bays, each roofed by a huge octagonal pyramid without window openings. One can imagine the effect of an interior thus strangely vaulted. These immense hollow pyramids, entirely *dark* at their summits, give a feeling of indefinable terror. A fourth pyramid, surrounded by four small belfries, crowns the square central tower, and around this tower are grouped the short transepts and the apse. The glimpse of the interior as seen from the porch is strange indeed. The dark nave serves as a frame to the centre of the church, which is bathed in a ghostly white light, while behind it is seen the apse lighted by rose-coloured windows.

The entire upper city is tunnelled with miles of subterranean passages connecting the château, the church, the donjon, and the walls. As one walks through the winding, twisting streets of this strange *ville haute*, black openings suddenly yawn at one's feet, or one looks into mysterious passages with ends lost in obscurity—reminders of hidden plots and intrigues. The deep moats are now filled with stables and houses or are planted with rows of linden trees. They say that the entire hill upon which Loches is built is honeycombed by enormous quarries, from which building stone was taken. I myself walked through two miles of them, and all along the path innumerable tunnels opened to right and left. One can thus go down even as far as the lower city, where one still finds old houses of the Renaissance and two of the beautiful gates of the outer wall.

III

CLIFF-DWELLERS

WE are accustomed to think of cliff-dwellers as a prehistoric race, the remains of whose few scattered dwellings are a matter of curiosity to tourists and a prize to antiquarians.

We had seen in Normandy isolated instances of people living in habitations half house and half cave, but they were of the very poorest class. So our first real cave-city came as a surprise, suddenly, at Rochecorbon, only a few miles from Tours.

High above us towered a huge mass of overhanging rock, strata upon strata, bearing upon its summit a most peculiar tower, supposedly a watch-tower in ages gone by. Its foundations hung over the rock upon which they were built, and it seemed as though the whole mass might crash down at any moment upon the village beneath.

THROUGH THE FRENCH PROVINCES

Habitation upon habitation could be seen scattered over the face of this cliff, doors and windows, narrow stairways and little belvederes, huddled in most picturesque disorder. Walls along the high-road hid the immediate foreground, and we looked in vain for an opening through which to have a nearer view of this strange community. At last we found a gate, and, peeping through, were greeted by a little old woman whose wrinkled, smiling face was surmounted by a snowy cap. Her doorway was a bower of flowers: hollyhocks, asters, nasturtiums, and deep June roses. By its side was an old well and a little out-house for her wood and gardening tools. Her cheery *"Bon jour"* was an invitation to enter, which we gladly accepted. We followed her across the little yard and were soon seated in her one and only room. This room was cosiness itself; a large canopied bed occupied the far corner; a great open fireplace filled one side, and around and on it were grouped all her lares and penates: her wedding-wreath—ah, so old!—her little crucifix, and china jars to hold her flowers. Photographs and tin-types of all her family and of her son in his soldier's uniform, a few cane chairs, a huge *armoire*, and a long, low chest completed the

Towered a huge mass of overhanging rock

furnishing of this little home. Spotless muslin curtains hung in the tiny windows and tempered the glaring red of the geraniums placed on the sill outside. Our hostess was only too glad to tell of her life and her home. Our first thought was that these caves must be damp and unsanitary. She told us, however, and we afterward found that her opinion was shared by all cave-dwellers, that these houses are, on the contrary, very dry and healthful. Certainly, if we may judge by the number of old people whom we saw living in them, they do not shorten the lives of their occupants. The peasants say, too, that they are cool in summer, and in the winter moderate the cold so that a fire is scarcely necessary.

Houses built at the foot of the hills are inclined to be damp, but those cut high up on the hillside are extremely dry and mould is never known in them. These upper caves are reached by special staircases cut in the face of the cliffs, and if the houses have more than one story, the stairs still continue to ascend its facade to reach the upper floor!

Sometimes these queer homes are superposed one upon the other, each approached at a different angle by its individual stairway. Often the only light is

A Cliff-dwelling

through the door, though there is usually a small square window, and frequently, when the house is built in an abrupt angle of the cliff, it has as many as four and five windows.

The long chest of which I have spoken is found in every dwelling, and is used for provisions. In it are kept the great loaves of bread which feed the little ones, the butter, cheese, and *confitures*, if the family is well-to-do. The vegetables are brought from the little garden, for each house possesses one; and if it be cherry season or grape time the good peasants will proudly offer you their prized fruits. But the comfort of the home is the open fireplace, wherein always hangs the great iron pot, blackened with the smoke of years. The peasants rarely have a match; if the fire be dead they go with a shovel to their neighbour and return with embers, as in the days of yore. There is always a well not far off, whose opening is closed with a little locked door, so that no one can use the water save those entitled to do so.

The rents paid for these little homesteads are really amusing; five dollars a year and you have a snug little place with a garden in front, and a view—oh, such as Monsieur le Comte in his château below cannot boast of. Eight dollars a year and you have a house of three or four rooms, with a stable and a store-house in a great cave not far off.

A place that had great charm for us was bought outright for twenty dollars! To think of providing a shelter for a lifetime at such a price! The owner, fancying to enlarge her domain, purchased an adjoining garden for twelve dollars. In it she raises green peas, cauliflower, lettuce, beets, and carrots, and a number of cherry and apple trees give her their fruit. With the pears she makes a drink of which the peasants are very fond.

The animals are kept in stables, also cut in the rock, the mangers and water-troughs being hollowed out of the solid stone. In these dark interiors glimpses are caught of cows sleepily chewing their cud; of horses eating their evening meal; of donkeys, who loudly bray their welcome as the door is opened. The peasants tell us that in such stables the animals never suffer from heat or cold, as Mother Earth tempers the extremes of the outer world with her own genial warmth.

So are the caves near the surface, utilised, but another world exists in the great labyrinths, ancient quarries, which tunnel the hillsides to their very centres. Here strange trades are carried on, and here the wines, for which this country is famous, ripen and become mellow in their cool cellars. The high caves are used as ateliers for the drying of hemp and the making of linen, and many of the great rafters on which the hemp was hung still remain. Often these quarries are forty feet high at the opening and lead into an interior chamber nearly one hundred feet square, with rough columns left to support the great weight overhead. Sometimes a house is built within this darksome chamber, vine-clad and moss-grown, and to such a home many a peasant bride has been taken to spend her honeymoon.

The strangest of these underground worlds which I visited was one devoted to the raising of mushrooms. Its limits seemed unbounded, as indeed they were, for it pierced the hillsides in every direction. We entered through an opening under an orchard of cherry trees. About ten feet inside the entrance was a well, and near it a lantern, which my kind guide lighted. We had proceeded but a few steps when suddenly the air became very close and warm and a dense white mist shut us in. I found this was heat and steam rising from huge piles of manure, stacked in an adjoining passage. When brought from the cavalry barracks near by, it is here "worked" by the

A Cliff-dweller's Home

admixture of water until it attains the required consistency. We soon passed this steam and heat and entered caves where the air was dry and cool.

Here manure is laid out in rounded hummocks along the walls, and in the wider passages, in lines down the centre as well. Sometimes there are as many as five of these rows. The mushroom seed is then placed in these manure piles, and the date of the "planting" is written on the wall above the section. The mounds are then covered with a fine powder obtained by sifting the tailings from the quarried limestone, just as coal dust is separated from coal. The mushroom is now planted and the hummock is left undisturbed for three months, more or less, when the first growth begins to appear. The mushrooms continue to sprout during three months, but then engender a certain poisonous gas which kills their own seed. The whole planting must then be removed and the place thoroughly cleaned.

During "harvest time" a crop is gathered every twenty-four hours. Three men with their great baskets, make the rounds of this underground farm every morning, and every day in the year can count on an immense crop which they ship to the large cities near by, and even miles away.

IN THE LAND OF THE TROUBADOURS

IN THE LAND OF THE
TROUBADOURS

JUST south of Limoges, in the Périgord, on the
line that connects Périgueux itself to Brive,
still stands the fine old castle of Hautefort,
crowning a rocky height and commanding a far-
reaching panorama. In this eyrie, remodelled into
a spacious château at a later day, was born the famous troubadour Bertrand de Born, whose rôle in the
history of the twelfth century was a conspicuous one.
He was the most complete expression of the epoch in
which he lived—a typical troubadour, son of the land
that placed the pretty arts of verse-making on a par
with valour in feats of arms. Nothing was sacred to
him. Family ties counted as naught. Twice he
drove his own brother from his castle that he might
himself remain sole lord. Through his intrigues he
arrayed Prince Henry of England against his unhappy
father, and induced the young English princes to
wage their parricidal wars.

Dante pictures him in hell wandering about carrying his head severed from his body. When Ber-

House at Sarlat where Etienne de la Boëtie was born

trand approached the rock whereon the poet stood, he raised on high his head, held like a lantern at arm's-length, that his words might better be heard, and thus he spoke:

IN THE LAND OF THE TROUBADOURS

"Thou who, still in the world of the living, comes to view the dead, behold my sorry plight! That thou mayest carry news of me back to earth, know that I am that Bertrand de Born who gave evil counsel to the young king. I made father and son enemies. And for the reason that I separated two beings so closely linked by nature, I now carry, alas, my brain separated from its motive which is the remainder of my body."

His poems were remarkable for their fire and violence, sometimes satirical, directed against the barons, sometimes martial, in honour of his royal friend Richard Cœur de Lion (it was Bertrand that dubbed him Richard Yea and Nay—oc e no), and sometimes amorous, in honour of the lady of his heart, Maenz, wife of Talleyrand de Périgord and daughter of the Viscount of Turenne.

This latter nobleman was, perhaps, the best-known patron of the troubadours, and at his castle, two of whose giant towers we visited not long ago, topping a hill just south of Brive, poets were always sure of a welcome.

Bertrand was the type of the more northern or Limousin school of minstrelsy, virile, strong, and contrasting sharply with the bards of the southland who, cradled in a more enervating air, sang a sweeter song. Such was the "tres gaye compagnie des sept troubadours de Tolose et mainteneurs du gay scavoir," protected by the powerful counts of Toulouse.

At this city in the Capitole, the Académie des Jeux Floraux, as it is called, still holds a meeting in the Salle de Clemence Isaure every three years, on May 3d, to contest for poetical prizes: a golden amaranth, a silver violet, wild rose, and marigold—laurels highly prized by the Gascon bards.

Richard the Lion Heart, friend of poets and himself a minstrel of no mean talents, spent much of his turbulent youth in this his duchy of Guyenne, and the whole country teems with recollections of him. At Martel his elder brother died penitent just after he had sacked the rich sanctuaries of Rocamadour near by to pay his Brabançons—a fact to which many of the faithful attributed his untimely end. And at the castle of Chalus, just beyond Limoges, Richard received his own death wound from the bow of Bertrand de Gourdon.

At all the castles in the valley lands and on the craggy hill tops tales of him are told, his hair-breadth

On every crag is perched a feudal castle

escapes, his magnanimity to his enemies, and his loyalty to his friends forming the theme of many a tra-

The medieval vision of Beynac seated on its proud cliff

dition. His friends, too, were all devotion to him. Is it not told of Blondel de Nesles, another poet of Languedoc, that he searched all Germany for his royal comrade when he was the captive of Leopold of Austria, and finally found him by singing a romance that they had composed together—a pleasing fiction, to be sure, but not altogether substantiated by history.

.   .   .   .

It is a very interesting country, this land of the troubadours, and surprisingly little known.

To one who is accustomed to think of France only as "sunny France," who pictures but the broad pastures of Normandy, the smiling beaches of Deauville and Dinard, the vineyards of Burgundy, the rich gardens of Touraine, the sunshine of the Midi, it would be a revelation, indeed, to traverse this south-west portion of the country—this *pays perdu* of the Limousin, the Périgord, the Cantal, and the Quercy.

From the mountains of Auvergne—the little Switzerland of France—a plateau, vast and monotonous, stretches westward and southward, silent, wild, and savage to-day as it was in the middle ages. Heather and ferns, birches and chestnuts, cover its hillsides. In the distance the mountains of Auvergne, forbidding and gloomy, profile their jagged barrier, rising and falling in peaks and domes. Here and there little lakes and swamp lands impart a sweetly melancholy note. Tiny streams issuing from these ponds cut for themselves narrow beds, deeper and deeper, through the ledges, finally swelling into torrents

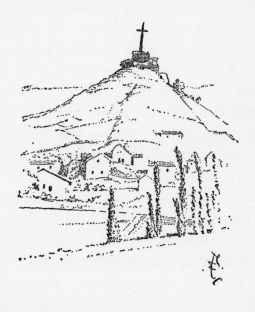

Vers

rushing in cascades down slaty gorges. Little by little these cañons enlarge to form a vast granite plateau once the bed of the Jurassic Sea, but now constituting the drear reaches of the Causse, sadder even than the upper Segala—a rocky table-land dried by the ardent sun and dotted only here and there with stunted oaks whose roots cling for life in the crevices. Its sole water-courses flow in a subterranean world, and can only be seen at the risk of one's life by descending into deep caverns whose narrow orifices open below into great halls polished by running waters and into chambers hung with stalactites reflected in murky pools.

Now and then a dolmen silhouettes its dark profile against the sky where the wild thyme perfumes the evening air. Human habitations are rare indeed. Great herds of sheep graze in these treeless plains, and they and the truffles for which the country is famous are the only riches of the *caoussenaous*—the peasants.

Into this Causse, in its savage splendour, rivers formed by these subterranean water-courses have now worn deep furrows which in time become valleys forming a happy contrast with their fertile fields and broad sheets of water reflecting tall files of poplars and giving life to villages crude and barbarous, it is true, but replete with vestiges of other days.

On every surrounding cliff or crag is perched a feudal castle or a pilgrim church. Franks and Visigoths, dukes of Aquitaine and lords of England, one after the other, have despoiled these river valleys to be followed by even more disastrous religious wars that tore brother from brother and drove peasants and villagers alike to refuge in fortified caves that are still to be seen loopholed in the cliffs on every hand.

Each succeeding master left his impress upon the land: a Gallic fort near Vers; a Roman arch of Diana at Cahors; relics of feudalism in castles, such as Beynac and Laroque, of the Renaissance, in superb châteaux like Cénevriers.

But here the story ends. Three centuries have elapsed and scarcely left a trace. The ruins are there, standing as on the morrow of their devastation, among rocks whose reddish tints at sunset seem still to reflect the glare of conflagration and along the banks of rivers whose saffron-tinted waters still seem to roll their floods of mud and blood.

At each turn of the road, and there are many, a new point of interest presents itself, now a ruined watch-tower perched solitary upon a hill top, now a giant crucifix planted upon a jagged rock, now an ancient church or dismantled castle with its vassal town clustered round its grass-grown moat, and ever and anon

glimpses of smiling meadows hemmed in by walls of
oölite and enriched by meanderings of the ruddy-
watered rivers.

All is smiling where the Dordogne rolls its waters
through a valley which is so easily reached from
Bordeaux, yet so seldom visited.

Stop first at Saint Emilion. From the station you
will see nothing. But climb the hill and you will discover for yourself, unknown to tourists, as quaint an
old town as you can find in many a long wandering
—a town of war-like aspect whose dismantled ramparts, pierced by numerous breaches; whose crumbling walls encircled by wide moats, evoke a past
filled with struggle and bloody combat. You will
find, too, within its gates, its royal castle and quaint
old houses and rock-paved streets, but besides it will
reserve for you a unique surprise hidden away in the
very bowels of the earth, its existence only betrayed
by a Gothic portal and some mullioned windows.

Yet enter this portal and you find yourself in an
immense monolithic church which has been pro-
nounced "the most singular in France and quite
unique in the world." And truly I know of none
like it, with its nave and aisles, its apse and altars,

its huge square pillars and soaring arches dug from the living rock way back in the dark ages by the patient hands of persevering monks, disciples of the

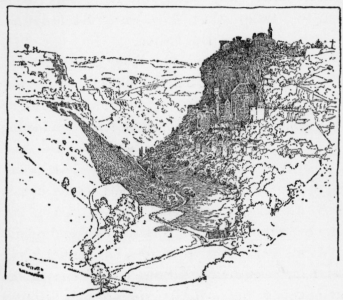

The Shadowy Vale of Rocamadour

saint who lived and died in the cave hard by. Six windows pierced in the hillside project into its aisles a pale, uncertain light which, before reaching the farthest extremities, is so attenuated that the arches cross in darkness and the eye can scarcely discern the altars rising in their shadowy niches and the tombs in their darksome chapels.

But a little beyond Saint Emilion, through the rich vineyards of the Bordeaux district, lies Bergerac—indelibly connected with Cyrano, "the demon of bravery"—made near and dear to all of us so recently by a troubadour of our own day. It is a pretty, smiling village, set in gardens hung with wistaria, and spreading its sunny quays along the river banks, very prosperous indeed, and quite bourgeois-looking—in no way recalling the peppery poet-swordsman.

Then the valley narrows, hemmed in by crags ribbed in courses like the massive rustic basements of giant castles. The houses throw up their roofs to steeper angles so the snow may slide away. We cross bridge after bridge over the meanders of the river, thrown from side to side by its rocky walls, and thread as many tunnels; then pass Saint Cyprien, climbing its steep hill-slope with cypresses leading in line to its church, and then, at twilight, come upon the mediæval vision of Beynac seated on its proud cliff, as perfect a type of feudal keep as one could hope to see.

We were to spend the night at Sarlat, and as we drove down the dark hill slopes from the station to the town, with the deep shadows of overhanging trees about us, I remembered that I had heard somewhere that wolves still abound in the vicinity and that not so very long ago one was killed in the streets of the town.

Sarlat is a fine old place with sombre, twisting streets lined with splendid stone houses, whose tall turrets and high-pitched slate roofs, and whose Gothic portals leading to spiral stairways evoke the heyday of its prosperity—the time of Louis XII and his immediate successors—perfect object lessons of the domestic architecture of the middle ages.

Here we were fairly in the land of the troubadours, and discovered on a pillar of the old city hall the following inscription placed there in 1908.

Aux Troubadours Elias Cairel, Aimeric de
Sarlat, Girault de Salignac, Lou
Bournat Bóu Périgord

Poets all of the Limoges school. This plaque was put up at a recent reunion of the Félibres, poets and writers of the Gascony country—the direct inheritors of the troubadours.

Sarlat has other claims to literary laurels. In a charming house fronting the cathedral church and

[143]

dating from the time of Francis I, Etienne de La Boëtie, Montaigne's lifelong friend, was born. The old town makes a charming centre for excursions. In the near vicinity lie the castles of Montfort and Fénelon, the latter, birthplace of many members of that illustrious house, remaining to-day a perfect specimen, intact, of a fifteenth-century stronghold.

Beyond lies Souillac, to which we made a special pilgrimage to see its byzantine church and the curious pillars of the west door adorned with sculptures of the greatest rarity, naïve, archaic in drapery and movement, and reminiscent only of the crude efforts of Northmen or the rude carvings of the Assyrians.

Beyond Souillac the Dordogne describes a sweeping bend around the Cirque de Montvalent, whose steep palisades, rising sheer from the river's bank, form a vast amphitheatre sheltering a number of picturesque old towns. Here lies Martel, where Prince Henry died of a fever in a house still pointed out and adorned with the leopards of England. And in the depths of these cliffs of Montvalent, which shore up the Causse de Gramat, lies the shadowy vale of Rocamadour, with its forgotten pilgrimage sleeping the sleep of the centuries.

A FORGOTTEN PILGRIMAGE

A FORGOTTEN PILGRIMAGE

THE Causse de Gramat is a rocky waste quite devoid of human habitation—here a little farm-house and there a primitive village, and if you asked how much the land was worth you would be answered, "Oh, about two francs a dog's run!" Its silence is that of the desert, save toward evening, when the stillness is broken by a long, far-away rumbling. This sound, strange as the country itself, is produced by the moving about of countless flocks of tawny-coloured sheep, with manes like lions, which graze among the little patches of stubby grass, carrying at their necks the *eskillo*—a heavy, cracked bell with a wild and uncouth note.

The horizon of the Causse is boundless. Now and then a dolmen is encountered and makes us think, as the evening shadows thicken, that white-bearded Druids will still meet here, and in the pale light of the moon offer their sacrifices and sing their psalms.

Suddenly, without a warning, in the midst of this wilderness, a chasm yawns at our feet—a huge cañon opens in the granite rock and a picture without parallel is presented to our astonished eyes. Far below is a shaded valley verdant with soft grasses and wooded with sycamores and beeches—the quiet valley of Rocamadour, so deep and so narrow that only the sun of mid-day penetrates to its green fields, while its trees grow tall and slender in their effort to reach the life-giving light.

It is impossible to describe the suddenness of the transition, the surprise of this unforseen oasis after the barren stretches and rocky reaches of the upper Causse. A river, the rippling Alzou, winds its long curves through this smiling valley, disappearing a moment under the briar bushes, only to appear again farther on near the tall poplars and dainty birches. But great cliffs hem in this charming Eden, and one precipitous rock, larger than all the rest, turns its scarred and battered face toward the rising sun.

Midway up its rugged sides clings a mass of masonry, square, buttressed, with steep slate roofs— more a fortress than a church—the shrine of Saint Amadour. No railroad's shriek, no tourist's caravan,

The Chapels

come to break the stillness of this far-away sanctuary, and its secret is to-day known only to the humble peasants who come to climb its holy stairs and bend the knee before the Black Virgin.

This is Rocamadour, the oldest and once the most venerated pilgrimage in all of France, visited by Saint Louis himself and many of his royal successors. By them its altars were enriched and its chapels built, and pilgrims came in thousands to participate in its miracles. But succeeding ages saw its glory fade, though even now, in our own generation, much has been done to restore its ancient grandeur.

A long, winding road gradually descends and brings us from the level of the upper plateau down to the village, which hugs the great rocks under the very foundation-stones of the sanctuaries. This road ends under a huge sycamore, whose base is encircled by a broad stone seat and whose spreading branches shelter a mossy stone crucifix. Here, in this little *place* overlooking the valley, the peasants gather in the cool of the afternoon, when the frowning mountains cast their long shadow far down over the valley. Here, too, is the blacksmith, and here we may see the patient oxen shod. We enter the town through a forti-

Procession on Ascension Day

fied gate—one of the four still spanning the road,—
once its means of defence, and then find ourselves in
the single village street, so narrow that two wagons
cannot pass, though such a necessity never arises in
Rocamadour! A few little shops, a so-called café,
a couple of comfortable hostelries contribute all the
life there is in the little town.

Midway between the two outer gates rises a broad
stone staircase, which leads to the sanctuaries above.
Many penitents climb these two hundred steps on
their knees, repeating an "Ave" on each step.
We saw a party of six, five women and a man, doing
this pious duty; the women kneeling, but the man,
too old and stiff to bend the knee, could but stand
and join in the responses.

A turn at the top of the stairs and we pass between
rows of shops in which holy mementoes and souvenirs are sold. Now we find ourselves in front of a great
Gothic doorway with a group of beggars before it.
A massive oaken double door, studded with huge
nails and strengthened with bands of wrought iron,
opens and gives access to a second staircase, which
tunnels its way under the dark foundation arches of
one of the largest buildings. Venders of rosaries and

Rocamadour from the River Alzou

crucifixes sit upon the steps knitting or talking to the pilgrims as they toil upward. A burst of light, a peep of blue sky above our heads, and we find ourselves in the *parvis*, surrounded on all sides by chapels.

Before ten a chorus of ringing bells fills the air, echoed by the bare cliffs on the opposite side of the cañon, and the echo is thrown back, only to be caught up again by a lustier ringing. The deep bells of the sanctuaries are chorded by the higher, clearer notes of the chiming from the nunnery. The sisters in long, black gowns descend the narrow path, the women in the village stop their work and begin climbing the long steps, muttering an "Ave Maria" and fingering their rosaries. The beggars take their accustomed places, arrange the placards about their necks, and jingle a sou in their tin cups as we pass. The bells swell in chorus and the rocks of the overhanging cliffs grumble back the tones. White-capped peasants bent double with age, old men in short blue blouses, young women in ribboned bonnets, brothers in long black gowns, and sisters in their flowing veils, enter the open door of the sanctuary and disappear in the darkness.

Rocamadour

A FORGOTTEN PILGRIMAGE

The bells cease their chiming. The great doors are closed, and there falls a hushed silence as the last vibrating murmur of the ringing ceases.

The beadle in his gorgeous costume of scarlet and gold paces back and forth on the upper balustrade— a guardian of peace—and the poor dog with his tail between his legs, who would follow his master to the very altar's foot, is hunted away by a gesture and a half-suppressed "*va-t-en.*"

I glanced about me at the chapels of the *parvis*, which form an irregular rectangle, their entrances on different levels. In front and up a short flight of steps is the chapel of the Virgin—a square Gothic edifice, whose corner is adorned with a delicate tourelle surmounted by a large figure of the Virgin. Near the entrance, painted on the exterior wall, is a strange old "Dance of Death," and near it, before entering the sanctuary, the peasants remove their hats and sing a quaint old *cantique*. The rough granite rocks form the entire west wall of the Virgin Chapel, and lighted candles of all sizes (votive offerings of pilgrims) are placed flaring against the uncut stone. The interior is full of mystery—dimly lighted and strangely disfigured by the irregularities of the jagged rock. The decorations add to the mystic effect—rich and deep in colour, with much ornament and gilding. High above the altar, enshrined in a canopy of gilt bronze, is the miracle-working statue of the Virgin and Child magnificently clothed, and said to have been carved in the first century by Saint Amadour or Zaccheus, who founded the sanctuary.

From this chapel a small door gives access to the Church of Saint Sauveur, the great square pile which is so conspicuous when seen at a distance. Its interior is grandly spacious and decorated with mementoes of the visits of many royal personages—Saint Louis, Charles IV, Louis XI, and others. Below this church, cut in the rock, is another of equal dimensions, the Chapel of Saint Amadour.

And now the voices in the church join in an anthem, the doors are thrown wide open, and a contented, God-fearing people form in groups as they come out. The gossips of the village vend their bit of news, the sisters speak a word of encouragement to the mothers, the brothers talk to their flock in merry groups or pause to bless a newly bought rosary or religious memento. I noticed among these chaplains one, conspicuous by his round, good-humoured face and

[156]

merry, dancing eyes, who seemed always surrounded by an eager group of devoted listeners. With his arm about one boy and his hand upon another's head, Monsieur Bonhomme (for so was he aptly named) was quite the ideal picture of a spiritual father. Soon, little by little, the place resumed its wonted, peaceful quietude.

A long, dark passage leads from the *parvis* to a strongly fortified gate, strengthened with all of feudal military art—crenelations, *mâchicoulis*, portcullis, and drawbridge The soldiers in the château above could reach the defences of this gate without being seen by the enemy, by means of a stairway of more than two hundred steps cut in the living rock. They could thus bear aid in the defence of the sanctuaries and of the treasures which they contained, during the long wars of the Middle Ages, when the whole country was infested with roving bands of lawless soldiers. To-day the stairs are only used by the brothers, descending from the clergy-house above, by aid of flickering candles, to repeat their matins and vespers.

In front of the great gateway ascends the *Chemin de la Croix*, a long, zigzag road with, at each turning, one of the fourteen stations, in the form of a little chapel, while at the end, on top of the great cliff, is a mighty wooden cross.

We are now on a level with the old château, the present residence of the chaplains, and recently re-modelled. It still retains, however, an ancient square tower and the old battlements. We may climb these latter to the *Chemin de Ronde*, and enjoy the magnificent panorama that spreads out at our feet. In three directions stretch the undulations of the interminable Causse, wilderness upon wilderness, cut here and there with long lines of stone fences. But as I looked over the fourth side, I caught my breath at the fearful drop into the valley below, and a cold, nervous shiver ran up my spine. I recall but one similar sensation, and that was when I peeped over the overhanging side of the Leaning Tower of Pisa. The eye becomes dizzy as it plunges down to the roofs of Spanish tile and chimney-pots far below—down, down into the fertile valley winding like a soft green river between its rocky walls, disappearing at the east as at the west in an abrupt turning of its course. Here on the battlements one may dream of times gone by, when the Sword went hand in

Crucifix in the Church of Saint Sauveur

hand with the Book and Belief was Strife. Now peace of conscience only reigns, and the low voices of the brothers come to us chanting the vespers, as the sun creeps behind the plateau throwing over the valley its long, forth-reaching shadows in a last embrace.

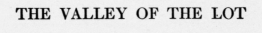

THE VALLEY OF THE LOT

THE VALLEY OF THE LOT

A LITTLE southward from Rocamadour, the Lot digs its way down from the mountains of Auvergne. With the intention of visiting its wild valley we motored on to Capdenac. A broad road, well paved as a city boulevard, lured us on—a road sometimes hewn in the solid rock, sometimes shored up on lofty viaducts, and at times tunnelling the hillsides, but always dominating the broad valley of the Lot, with its rows of stately poplars, its ripening fields and orchards, shut in on either hand by steep and jagged cliffs, rich and varied in colour, shading through the entire gamut of chrome, ochre, sienna, and russet brown.

And here, almost at the outset, we met our first "rabassiaire," with his pig, hunting for truffles. We knew we should find him hereabouts, for this, above all others, is his country.

In Provence truffles are good; they are better in Languedoc, Guyenne, and the Périgord, but the best

come from this very province of the Quercy, especially
from the environs of Cahors—Lalbecque, Limogne,
and Arcambal, being, as it were, the very Château
Yquem of truffledom.

With his pig hunting for truffles

The search for this most precious of vegetable
growths is the all-engrossing industry of the country
—an ungrateful industry, too, fickle as the caprices
of a woman. For ten or fifteen years a plantation
may be good, and the "caussenard" who owns it may
gain as much as four or five thousand francs a season
—an enormous sum for the country. Then, little
by little, the deposits grow less; the truffigène fly,

sure indicator of large bulbs, fails to appear, and the "caveur" or truffle-hunter's work is at an end.

Gone also is the occupation of the educated sow— the real "rabassiaire." Many animals are fond of truffles: the hare, the boar, and so is the dog, which is often trained to hunt them; but the real epicure, the animal who surely and quickly scents the dainty, is the pig, preferably the sow, which has been previously taught by hunting potatoes hidden in the ground with bits of truffle. When the pig's education is complete, a peasant leads it forth by a rope which he holds in one hand, while in the other he carries a pointed stick. As soon as the sow scents the dainty it becomes greatly agitated, quivering from head to foot, and starts to root, and then the peasant, rapping it sharply on the snout, quickly pulls it away and digs up the treasure. In Cahors, in Martel, and in Brive we saw important markets where truffles are the only commodity, and where the exchange of money from four to six on a Friday afternoon often amounts to ten or fifteen thousand francs.

We lunched at Cajarc, a dingy town topped by a picturesque old castle—a strange feudal conglomeration of towers, bastions, and curtain walls pierced by the tiniest of windows.

Of our *déjeuner* I remember but little, save that the hotel was most primitive; but that, perhaps, is true of

Cajarc

all inns in this forsaken country. Few and far between, indeed, are spots where the weary traveller may rest his head, as we were to find out for ourselves that very night.

[166]

THE VALLEY OF THE LOT

All the afternoon we drove against a head wind, and, tired and hungry at last, at about six o'clock reached Tour de Faure, but there forgot all fatigue in the contemplation of the glorious picture that opened before us. From the river's banks, which here swing round in a wide circle, a giant cliff rises, sheer and perpendicular as the Tarpeian Rock. On top of this precipice a village hangs—Saint Cirq-la-Popie—dwellings clinging, lichen-like, to any chink in a rock; gardens wherever there is a tiny parcel of earth; houses, gateways, walls, and towers consolidating with the crags on which they stand, the whole crowned by a charming old abbey-church whose apse, backing out high above the river, mirrors itself in the waters hundreds of feet below.

My handbook of the Touring Club of France told us there was an inn at Saint Cirq-la-Popie; in fact, even gave the prices, which I thought were rather too moderate. As we crossed the river bridge we encountered a priest and with him a shabby-looking individual. To make assurance two times sure, I inquired if they knew of a good hotel in St. Cirq. The priest and his companion exchanged a quick glance, and perplexity was plainly written on their faces.

A hotel in St. Cirq? Who ever heard of such a thing? No, they surely knew of none.

"But," said I, "how about this 'Cheval Blanc' that my book tells of?"

"Never heard of such a place," was the priest's reply. "The blacksmith has a room, I believe, but really, I think you would be better off down here by the station in that farm-house yonder."

The farm in question looked none too preposessing, so, thanking the priest, we decided to mount the hill and search for the mythical "White Horse."

In the village, as on the bridge, no one seemed to know of it. We wandered about the twisting alleys for a while, wriggling between houses, rocks, and caves, until finally we came upon the blacksmith in his grimy shop, opening on a little square, smelling of burnt hoofs and leather. He readily consented to show us his room, and led us—two unwilling wayfarers—up a flight of steps at the back of the smithy. Half-way up we paused, our heads just above the flooring of an evil-odoured room, dark, grimy, dingy; a bed in one corner, a chimneypiece in another, with, upon it, a drunken row of half-emptied liquor bottles; a table in the centre and a settle at either side—

Saint Cirq-la-Popie

guest-chamber, cabaret, living-room, dining-room, and kitchen all in one. Where could one find a better picture of life in the middle ages?

Pont Valentré, Cahors

This was the room in question, and one glance was enough. We opted for the house far below by the railroad track. So down we went again to the farm by the river.

It was now seven o'clock and we were hungry and desperate. A woman received us at the high gate of a spacious court-yard with stables and barns at one side, waggon-houses at the other, the inevitable manure pile with its brood of picking fowl in the centre, and the dwelling-house at the back.

Yes, she had room—her own room, in fact—that she would give up for the night. She showed it—none too lovely: colourless walls, a heavy beamed ceiling, a rough oak table whose greasy top plainly told that it frequently did duty at wedding-feasts, a bed with dingy curtains whose original colour and pattern had been obliterated by years of usage, a baby's crib with a child asleep within it!

If Monsieur and Madame would take a walk she would make all clean and prepare a dinner.

So at eight we sat down to a frugal meal, with the gruff voices of a crowd of men shouting politics in the next room over their glass of "petit bleu," and punctuating their arguments with many a resounding thump upon the table. This seemed likely to last all night.

When we went to our room with the feeble light of a single half-candle, we sat down in real despair. To be sure, the linen had been changed, the infant had disappeared, but oh! how we dreaded that old wooden bed with its dingy, shabby curtains!

Was nothing else to be done?

Then I remembered a smiling villa about a mile down the road smothered in flowers behind a high garden wall with fruit trees all about. If we went to the proprietor and explained our dilemma, might he

Barbreau and Tour des Pendus, Cahors

not know how to help us, or better still (and that was my secret hope), might he not take us in for the night?

So off we went and jingled the bell, which was answered in person by a kindly old gentleman whom we had seen taking his airing on the front steps. We stated our predicament and he, like the priest, remained perplexed. Finally he said: "I do know of

[171]

a nice room with some peasants—there down the road—the first big gate. Try it. Perhaps it may be vacant."

We entered a court hung with a grape-vine arbour, and in it, in the deepening twilight, we spied a woman —a giantess of mighty brawn, fit in figure, if not in face, to be a Brunhilde—balancing a horse-trough upon her head. As soon as she saw us, with a toss of her head she sent the unwieldy tub spinning into a corner, as if it had been a wicker basket, and quickly came forward to greet us.

To be sure she had a room—would we mount and see it?

An exterior staircase led to an upper porch whence a door gave access to a large chamber with three windows, a room possessing every advantage that the others had lacked: neat, with whitewashed walls and a rough but spotless floor; a cupboard with dishes in one corner; a chimney-piece decorated with a *bouquet de mariée* and tin-types of relatives mostly in soldier clothes; a bed with a fresh white coverlet knit by hand. Ah, here at last was a place to rest one's weary head! With no loss of time we went back to the public house, and with all possible delicacy (for the woman had been kind and done her best) told her of our decision.

On awaking next morning, our coffee, the bread, and especially the butter, were so good that we decided to spend the morning sketching at St. Cirq and return to lunch. The memory of that luncheon remains with us still, prepared with care, served with daintiness, and accompanied by a light but fragrant wine. The menu was the peasant woman's and showed no great originality, but what can one expect in the markets of a *pays perdu?* Then the table was cleared, the crumbs brushed away, and a cup of aromatic coffee comforted our nerves while we feasted our eyes upon the broad expanse of sunlit country, the fields of ripening grain, the heavy-laden fruit trees, the ruddy cliffs and Saint Cirq daringly perched, like an edelweiss, over the deep abyss.

In the afternoon we were off to Cahors. Still high above the wanderings of the Lot, we passed Conduché Saint Géry, Vers with its giant cross, Savanac, Arcambal, Laroque-des-Arcs, each in its way an evocation of the middle ages, and then spied far off on the horizon a vision of Cahors, capital of the Cadurci, lying on its rolling peninsula, encompassed and moated by a loop of the Lot.

Nor does the spell of the impression lessen as we approach the fine old capital of the Quercy. Before entering, you swing all round the town unfolding in rapid succession its picturesque declivities, punctuated with mediæval ruins, and spreading its tree-grown boulevards along the quays.

We found Cahors worth visiting if for no other reason than its Pont Valentré—a splendid fourteenth-century bridge spanning the Lot to the west of the town.

I shall never forget the picture it presented one summer morning as we lounged in a garden by the river and watched a regiment of lancers troop across it, the horses neighing, the steel helmets flashing in the sunlight, the lances with fluttering pennants atilt at a thousand angles, like knights of old faring forth to battle.

THREE OLD HILL-TOWNS OF GASCONY

THREE OLD HILL-TOWNS OF GASCONY

I

CORDES

THE traveller on the road to Toulouse, just
after passing through the wild valley of the
Aveyron, if he keep a sharp look-out, will
notice, in the distance to the left, rising above the in-
tervening hills, a city, strangely perched on an isolated
cone, piling upon the steep slopes its ruinous, red-
roofed houses and bearing, like an aigrette, upon its
summit, the belfry of its church. It is Cordes.

As we approach, its picturesqueness becomes more
and more apparent, until, as the last rolling hillside
is surmounted, the uniqueness of its situation and the
strange contours of its masses of mediæval masonry
are indeed remarkable.

Before us stretches a smiling, sunlit valley, perhaps three miles wide and as many long, through

which winds a swift-flowing river, the Céron. This valley is bounded on all sides by well-cultivated, gently sloping hillsides, rising in the form of an amphitheatre to the height of about four hundred feet. Just in the middle of this amphitheatre stands an abrupt hill, entirely isolated, its sharp declivity about the same on all sides, and on its top is perched the city of Cordes. How strange a site for a city, thus elevated above the land which forms its base, with its lowest walls raised to the level of the hill tops which bound the horizon, but separated from them by a natural moat, three hundred feet deep and a mile to two miles in breadth! Only one means of communication with the valley below is at first apparent—a steep, winding road, so steep as to be absolutely impassable for horses. We find afterward, however, that on the east side, the town has gradually descended the hillside by a zig-zag road and joined its suburb of La Bouteillerie in the valley below.

The reason for building a city in such a position is readily guessed. Cordes is old; its act of birth was written by Raymond VII, Count of Toulouse, in the early part of the thirteenth century, when he granted permission to the citizens of Saint Marcel, whose town

Cordes

near by had been pillaged over and again by roving bands of soldiers, to build upon this isolated hillside, whose natural defences are apparent even to the most unskilled eye.

The buildings were begun on the highest land, and important buildings they were too, for Cordes counted many wealthy citizens. To protect them, a great encircling wall was built, with two gates, both of which yet remain, though in ruins—one toward the west, the Porte des Houmets, the other facing the east, the Porte des Roux. Only two streets traverse the town between these gates, and in the centre, on the very apex of the hill, is the market-place. Here has always been the focus of the city life, and with this market-place most of the history of Cordes is connected.

The Book of Iron

Twelve years after the foundation of the city, when the Council of Toulouse had just established the Inquisition, Cordes saw three *frères prêcheurs* enter her walls, and a few days after an old woman was burned for heresy in the market-place. Another execution was about to follow when the people arose, killed the inquisitors, and threw their bodies in the city well. The Pope, not receiving satisfaction for this misdeed, excommunicated the city, and it remained under his ban for nearly a hundred years, when a solemn ceremony was held and the Papal Bull was revoked. The Pope ordered the city well to be walled up, and an iron cross, which still stands near one of the pillars of the market-place, was erected over it, and to this day we read, on one of the flagstones near by, "*Ici est un puits de cent mètres de profondeur.*

During this stormy period in the life of Cordes, when her citizens showed such a strong will of their own, the *libré ferrat* (as it was called in *patois*) was written. It is an ancient book, written on parchment by the monks as only the monks could write, and engrossed with ornamental capitals and exquisite borders. It is bound in leather, richly tooled, and strengthened with nails and rivets, and with heavy iron corners and brass clasps. It was attached by means of a chain to one of the pillars of the market-place. Its first part consists of the Book of the Gospels, on which all oaths were taken; then follow, in detail, the laws and customs of Cordes. The book was public property, and all—rich and poor alike—could consult it at any time and settle their disputes. As I fingered its well-thumbed pages with my friend the *archiviste*, he pointed out some of its curious clauses, written in the *patois*—a corruption of Spanish and French—which still prevails in the south-west of France. One, for instance, tells that at Christmas-tide, the heads, feet, and tail of all animals killed should revert as tithes to the lord of the manor.

A By-way

In the sixteenth century the market was roofed over. Twenty-four stone pillars were built to support the massive roof-beams, and until recently there was also a granary above. One of the pillars is hollow and

[181]

was used as a measure, the grain being let into it from the upper store-house, and when the column was full the purchaser filled his sack from a tap at the bottom. The market is smoothly paved in flagstones, and has always served as the place of meeting for local re-unions, and now, to the tune of the flute and violin, the merry men and maidens, arm in arm, dance on the historic well, whose presence cost their forefathers such sore distress.

Saturday is market day. Then the peasants gather from all the country round, and toil up the steep hill to arrange their wares in and about the *place*. Here they barter and trade while the townsfolk lay in their weekly provision. Farmer's wives carry long white sacks into which they put their purchases, tying a knot over each article, so that finally the bag has the appearance of a long string of Frankfurt sausages. The country people bring well-filled baskets of luncheon, and at eleven o'clock regale themselves on good bread and cheese, a bottle of the sparkling wine of Gaillac, and a big piece of salted goose. The salted goose is a famous dish, and its abundance in Cordes is easily accounted for. *Pâté de foie gras* is a staple product, and of course necessitates the fattening and killing of many geese. After the liver is removed the fowl must be put to some use, so the meat is salted, and really makes a very appetizing dish served with large, fresh brown beans.

After the busy hours of the market, quiet settles over the old town, and, as I sit sketching, I recognise the familiar sounds of the humdrum daily life: the trades-people working in their shops; the shuttle of the loom, as the weaver throws it back and forth—clack, clack as the frame falls after each thread is passed; the creak of the treadle as the wife winds the bobbin; the fall of the hammer as the shoemaker drives in each hobnail until the sole is quite covered and ready to aid some brave man or woman to climb the slippery, rock-paved streets; the sound of the saw, as old *père* Aurillac (who is ninety and bent double with the burden of his life) cuts in pieces the pile of wood which I watched him carry up the hill on his back—a load so large that it almost completely hid him for only his poor faltering feet were visible.

In the Grande Rue are most of the great houses—seven of them, all more or less similar in style and strangely reminiscent of the palaces on the Grand Canal in Venice. They are beautiful specimens of the domestic architecture of the thirteenth century. The ground-floor of each façade is composed of a series of Gothic arches. The first and second floors are pierced by two or three openings, each composed of several windows, whose pointed arches repose on clustered columns with foliated capitals of exquisite design. Most of the sculpture is lavished on these windows or on the string-courses which run across the design at the bases of the window-openings and the spring of the arches. Quadrupeds, birds, figures, walk upon these courses or decorate their extremities—whole scenes of the hunt embellishing one house.

As the city increased in size, the original nucleus inside the topmost wall grew too small for its needs and jumped over the barrier; so a new rampart was built, only to be succeeded by another and another, each enclosing a larger area than its predecessor, until the inner city was surrounded by a quintuple wall pierced by more than fifty gates, many of which yet remain. The town has never overlapped the fifth wall, below which the hill slopes remain a succession of grain-fields and vineyards with the cemetery, cypress-grown, clinging close to the lowest western wall.

THREE OLD HILL-TOWNS OF GASCONY

One day I saw a funeral winding its way to the little grave-yard through a dark and narrow street—

Stairway of the Pater Noster, Cordes

so dark, indeed, that the candles carried by the altar-boys shone clearly in the midday light, and so narrow that, to let it pass, I must needs take refuge in a door-way. Ahead walked the priest chanting, with the choir-boys; then the bier carried by hand—three stalwart men on each side, for the town's thorough-fares are so steep that no hearse drawn by horses could be led through them. It was a strange and im-pressive sight—impressive from its utter simplicity—with the long train of black-robed mourners—the men and then the women hobbling along over the rough rock pavements.

The streets of the town, if such they may be called, for they are more like by-ways, backing and twisting on themselves, or following the old *chemins de ronde* by the dismantled ramparts, are crowded with half-ruined houses, many of them rearranged from fine old buildings. Ugly little modern windows have been opened in the corners of beautiful casements of the Renaissance; Gothic windows *en croix* have been entirely walled up, and near them grin fantastic gar-goyles strangely mutilated.

One interesting by-way, leading to the Tour de l'Horloge, is called the Stairway of the Pater Noster. A chapel, belonging to the Brothers of St. Joseph, stood near the head of the steps. At their base was the residence of the brothers, so that in going to and from service they climbed the stairs, of which there are just the same number as there are words in the pater noster. Thus, by saying one word on each step, the prayer could be finished when the top or bottom was reached.

To-day the town is sleepy and almost devoid of activity, and its population has dwindled from three thousand to eighteen hundred souls. Created for struggle and resistance in a time of bloody quarrels, Cordes could only maintain her importance in more peaceful, commercial ages by coming down from the summit to which she owed her originality and her strength. This she has refused to do. Now the railroad has left her isolated, so that she has entered upon a period of long and incurable decay which will eventually leave her a mere ruin, proudly perched on her far-away hill top.

II

ALBI

THE little local train had just traversed an un-interesting stretch of meadow-land when the huge red mass of the Cathedral of Albi loomed into view—a mass most imposing in size, but not picturesque when viewed thus over the flat grain-fields.

From the station I hurried through a succession of modern French provincial streets, some attempting to be boulevards by lining up their rows of young plane trees, dotting the dazzling roadway with their scanty shade, others filled with ill-stocked shops and paved with the roughest cobbles. Soon, however, the streets narrowed; the houses took on a quainter aspect, huddled closer together for mutual support and protection, thrust out their upper stories on heavy corbels, and raised their roof-lines into pointed gables and high-peaked dormer-windows; and finally an abrupt turning brought me into the market-place.

[188]

THREE OLD HILL-TOWNS OF GASCONY

It was nine in the morning, and the market was at its height—and such a market!—one of those southern marts, where every bright colour is displayed at once,

The Cathedral and Archbishop's Palace, Albi

where every heap of gray-blue cabbages and every pile of rich red berries and golden apricots is sheltered by an umbrella of a different hue—green, red, blue, purple—where every woman wears a bright kerchief or a knot of gay ribbon. And such a clatter of tongues, and such animation! How interesting the coifs! The old women in little, close-fitting caps, with wide double ruffles round the face, framing it in an aureole of white; the young women with their hair bound in gay plaid kerchiefs, covered by large straw hats of curious fashion, with low crowns bound by wide bands of velvet ribbon.

Behind this animated scene, brilliant in the glare of the hot southern sun, towers the red-brick apse of the Cathedral of Saint Cecilia. Half-way up to its roof-line, thick and solid walls, devoid of detail, seem by their threatening masses to defy all attack, and fill the mind

A Side Street, Albi

Albi Cathedral from the Market

with a feeling of mysterious fear. The upper half
of these gigantic walls is pierced by long slits
of windows, like loopholes, and the entire church,
from basement to balustrade, is strengthened by
round, tower-like buttresses, so that one is tempted
to ask, "Is this a fortress—is it a church?" As we
look at the crenelated portal of Dominique-de-Flor-
ence, it, too, is a castle gate, though decorated with
statues of the Virgin and saints. But beyond it we
catch a glimpse of the marvellous baldaquin of the
south portal in the richest flamboyant Gothic, and
we say that surely must be the entrance to a temple
of God. The interior leaves no vestige of doubt in the
mind—its soaring arches, its chapels, its delicate
frescoes of the Last Judgment, with Giotto-like figures
moving in landscapes of rare simplicity; its rood-
screen, whose stone is as delicately wrought as a piece of
Valenciennes lace, and whose canopied niches are peopled with countless statues and enriched with traceries
so intricate that the mind is appalled at the power of imagination that conceived them—all tell us that it is religious faith alone which has accomplished such marvels.

Around the cathedral wind the crooked little streets
of the old city which sought protection under its

frowning walls and encircling ramparts—a twisting labyrinth of by-ways and alleys where the sun seems to bestow its rays regretfully—streets so narrow as to be quite impassable for wagons, and in which passers-by are suddenly seen in a ray of sunshine as it squeezes between the tall buildings, and then are swallowed up completely in the darkness beyond.

But the place we liked best to linger in was across the Tarn in the suburb of La Madeleine. There in a garden, under the shade of a group of locust trees, sitting in the cool, tall grasses, we passed the late afternoon hours. And what a view to look upon! Below us the broad river flows lazily by. Across it the steep hillside is shored up by long arcaded embankments, each supporting a lovely garden, whose flowers, trellises, and clambering vines glow in the warm sunshine. Groups of houses with rich ochre walls, bright green shutters, little iron-railed balconies and red-tiled roofs string their irregular course along the bluffs, ending in the prison-like mass of the archbishop's palace. Above, dominating all this rustic beauty, towers the glorious mass of the cathedral, its lofty west tower gorgeously transfigured by the setting sun, glowing like a coral in all the

A Lane, Albi

shades of red from shell-pink to richest crimson, detaching its luminous mass from the deep-blue sky.

After the heat of the summer day, a delicious coolness comes to refresh the sun-beaten town, and every door and window is flung wide open. Each occupant abandons his four walls to inhale a breath of fresh air and to seek simple amusement on the promenade. Here giant sycamores and chestnuts interlace their century-old branches in a vaulted canopy and a darkness lowers: a veiled mystery, born of the approaching night, enveloping the shadowy avenue. The massive tree trunks—vague yet mighty columns— become solid walls as they disappear in far perspectives to the city lights twinkling in the distance. Scattered among the trees glow coloured lanterns. Here a glint catches the falling waters of a fountain, lighting the sparkling jets of crystal; there a gleam falls full upon white-gowned maidens as they walk arm in arm, or touches the red epaulets and white gloves and spats of the soldiers. The clear voices of young people ring out in merry laughter; mothers tend their babes in arms; workmen drag their heavy-nailed boots as they shuffle along, while old *rentiers*, showing ample expanses of white waistcoat, lean heavily on their canes as they grumble their deep-rooted convictions to their companions. Gay *kiosques* blaze out their attractions; shooting-galleries and wheels of fortune, alluring chances in all sorts of seductive lotteries, make easy game of the soldiers. The military band blows forth its lustiest notes, and young and old forget their daily toil for bread—forget their burdens borne in the mid-day sun—and are happy in the night shadows under the spreading branches.

III

CARCASSONNE

WE may have read much of the Cité of Carcassonne and seen many photographs of its walls and towers, yet we do not seem in any way prepared, in our latter-day civilisation, for the strangeness of aspect of this mediæval city, crowning the rolling hills upon which it is built, with the silhouette of its double line of ramparts and the profile of its innumerable, slate-roofed towers of irregular size, its crenelated castle and fortress church. When I first visited it years ago, Carcassonne was comparatively little seen by tourists and the old cité had no hotel.

And that was a pity, for one who spends a day or two in wandering along its well-kept *chemins de ronde*, on whose broad flagstones the spurred heels of steel-clad knights still seem to ring; or peeps

through the long slits of the *meurtrières* or down the
abysses of the machicolations; or climbs the winding stairs of its turrets, cunningly guarded by doors
at unlooked-for angles, will come away with an ob-

The Upper City, Carcassonne

ject lesson in feudal warfare which will light up the
pages of history with a new interest. Every detail
of barbacan and portcullis, of drawbridge and pos-
tern-gate, of *hourds* and *volets*—every cunning sys-
tem of attack and defence from the strong but ill-laid
masonry of the Visigoth to the perfections of Saint

Louis and Philip the Rash, can here be studied from the life.

It takes but little imagination to people the silent streets of the Cité with armoured crossbow men, to see the populace rushing to the walls to pour boiling oil and hurl the very masonry of their houses upon the soldiers of the King.

After its redoubtable defences were completed, this virgin city was never taken, for, during the whole period of the middle ages, when all the south-west of France was ravaged by the wars with England, and city after city was attacked and taken by Edward the Black Prince, the Cité of Carcassonne alone was deemed impregnable and only gave itself up when all of Languedoc had fallen before the conqueror.

Now from the top of the beetling walls one looks over smiling valley lands—vineyards and orchards— far over to the sombre Montagne Noire on the one hand and to the snow-clad peaks of the Pyrenees on the other. Below and near by flows the River Aude, spanned by its twelfth-century bridge, and on its far bank we descry the new city of Carcassonne, itself six hundred years old and to-day a commercial town of some importance.

THREE OLD HILL-TOWNS OF GASCONY

Within the walls of the old upper city, the narrow little streets are almost deserted—a few old women knitting or gossiping in the cool corners, a cat slink-

The Porte Narbonnaise, Carcassonne

ing along in the tiny shadows of the high southern sun. It was one of those first hot June days when I wandered through these little lanes as the noon hour approached, seeking to make arrangements for my lunch, so that I might be spared the descent of the long hill to my hotel in the new town. A turning of the street brought me before a café, but there I was told that they served no meals. Just beyond, in the Rue de l'Aude, I met the wife of the *concierge* of the fortifications, a fresh-looking, kindly-faced woman, to whom I explained my dilemma. But no, there was no place where Monsieur could dine. I hinted—yes, it *was* a hint, and I confess it—that all I wanted was a bit of bread, an egg, and a salad, and she took the cue by saying, "*Pardi*—I can provide *that*, if Monsieur is not too *exigeant*." So we entered a neat little house, where I busied myself looking at photographs until lunch was announced.

My cover was laid at a round table in the corner of the kitchen, with the custodian himself beside me and his wife across the table. But instead of the meagre meal which I had suggested, I found prepared a veritable little feast. The "best linen" was on the table, which was arranged with care, and on it were carefully disposed a rosy dish of radishes, fresh olives, sliced *saucisson d'Arles*, a pickled mackerel, and cold ham. Monsieur filled my glass with a charming grace and asked me to sample his wine, for it would be of

special interest to me, having been grown on the very
ramparts of Carcassonne! Yes, the little vineyard
was just in front of the church of St. Nazaire, and
they pressed the wine themselves. The sausage, too,
proved to be native-born, and the ham was its own
brother, for they were made from two little white pigs
which the custodian himself had raised the winter
before! So the luncheon passed—the eggs, the *toma-
tes farcies* cooked in olive-oil and served in an earthen
dish, the fresh, crisp salad, *roquefort*, and fruits—rel-
ished with a running fire of small talk and anecdote
from my host and hostess. Then the coffee was
ground in a little mill before my eyes, its delicious
aroma filling the air, and served strong and hot.
An hour later, when, as I rose to say good-bye, my
hand strayed toward my pocket, the good wife lifted up
her hands and cried, *"Mais, Monsieur, vous plaisan-
tez!"* Happy people who have enough to give some
away, and take in and feast a perfect stranger at their
board—kindly folks of the Midi with their warm
southern temperament, who carry, as my host ex-
pressed it, their hearts within their hands!

THE VALLEY OF THE RHONE

THE VALLEY OF THE RHONE

WE have now, at Carcassonne, come within sight of the Pyrenees—which means the southern border of France—so it now behooves us to choose an itinerary for the return journey. The evident and, indeed, the best thing to do, is to swing around (a rather long motor drive of about one hundred and eighty miles or a day in the train) through the old province of Languedoc to Provence.

The first leg of this journey takes us to Narbonne, rival of Marseilles in the days of Roman supremacy and perhaps the wealthiest city in all of ancient Gaul, but now reduced to a busy enough provincial town with wide boulevards and crowded cafés and quite cut off from the sea that once laved its wharves and was the great source of its riches.

A long, straight sweep of dazzling white road leads on to Beziers, which finally piles itself upon a hill before us, a mass of towers and crowded houses with red-tiled roofs, but making a more picturesque impression when viewed from a distance that it does upon closer scrutiny. It possesses, however, a cathedral of some interest with, near it, a terrace that commands a fine and far-reaching panorama of the blue silhouettes of the Cevennes on the one hand and of the still deeper blue waters of the Mediterranean upon the other.

Between Beziers and Montpellier one has a vision, off to the right, of Cette on a narrow spit of land, like Cadiz, gleaming white between a sapphire sea and an azure sky. Montpellier, set in the heart of an important viticulturist region, is, to the French, known as a famous university town, from whose colleges have graduated many men of distinction and world-wide reputation. It has an exceptionally beautiful promenade, the Peyrou, adjoining which is one of the oldest *jardin des plantes* in France—a luxuriant garden of exotic plants laid out, way back in the sixteenth century, by order of King Henry of Navarre.

Another long stretch of level road takes us on toward Nimes. Here we really enter Provence, that land of poetry, legend and romance sung, in its own strange language by Mistral, then by Félix Gras and Alphonse Daudet, "most sane and sympathetic of realists," who, in "Les Lettres de Mon Moulin," "Numa Roumestan" and "L'Arlesienne" and, above all, by his bombastic pictures of Tartarin de Tarascon, has made these volatile people of the Midi almost as familiar to us as our own and their country a haunt of the fancy even to those who have never seen it.

Each town has its legend or its story. For instance, as we entered Lunel, we recalled that its people have long been popularly known as "Pesca Luna," fishers of the moon. If you asked why, you would be told that tradition has it that some idiots of this town were one evening trying to catch the moon in a bucket as it was reflected in the waters of the canal. When the bucket touched the water, however, the moon danced about and the onlookers cried, "Look out or it will get away." So, when the water was still again, the simpletons lifted the bucket very slowly and very carefully and started for town with the moon in the bucket. Unfortunately, however, upon the way they stopped at a tavern for a drink and a donkey, passing by, saw the bucket by the door, gulped down the water and, no doubt, with it, the moon!

. . . .

I am not going to tarry in Nimes, nor, indeed, do

THROUGH THE FRENCH PROVINCES

I mean to more than allude to the beauty of the cities of Provence for other books (and many of them) have been devoted to this delightful region.

Avignon, City of the Popes

Nîmes with its Roman ruins and its chaste and beautiful Maison Carrée, perhaps the most perfect Roman edifice remaining outside of Italy; the imposing Pont du Gard near by; Aigues Mortes, whose stern battlements and towers, still standing without a breach, looked down upon St. Louis as he departed for the Crusades; Arles, with its celebrated amphitheatre, its curious Musée Arlaten and its remarkable church of Saint Trophime; Avignon, City of the

Popes, with its bridge famed in song and story—
each one of these cities with its fascinating back-
ground of history and its lovely surrounding country,
may well tempt the leisurely traveler for a stay of
some length.

But let us hasten on up the Valley of the Rhone
for, before terminating this volume, I want to introduce to the reader one more of the French Provinces
that, thus far, has almost entirely escaped the attention of the traveler.

Our road thus takes us on to Orange where we
must stop long enough to see the Arch of Marius and
the great Roman theatre in which the Comédie Française gives performances from time to time. And as
we visit the ruins of the castle of the Counts of
Orange above this theatre, how many of us, I wonder, will connect these tottering ruins with William
of Orange, that proud and silent King of England,
who, nevertheless, drew his principal title from this
now obscure city of Provence.

Beyond Orange, we follow the banks of the Rhone
with the hazy blue outlines of the Cevennes to the
westward. A succession of romantic landscapes ac-
company us as we speed along, passing in turn over

the long, long bridge of the Holy Spirit, the beetling ruins of Rochemaure's ancient castle, the picturesque mass of Lavoulte-sur-Rhone and the abbey church of Tournus, where Saint Valerian preached. Then we arrive at Vienne where we must see the Temple of Augustus, erected soon after the beginning of the Christian era by the Emperor Claudius and owing its remarkable state of preservation to the fact that, at an early date, it was converted into a Christian church.

Lyons will be our next objective and thence we follow the west bank of the river as far as Macon, where, by the way, there is an excellent hostelry in which to pass the night.

At this point, instead of continuing on to Beaune and Dijon, as is usually done and so, through the heart of Burgundy to Paris, I should counsel our last detour. By taking the road to Autun, a few miles beyond Macon, we reach Cluny where still stand the extensive buildings of the celebrated Benedictine monastery whose abbots were as powerful as any in France and one of whom, indeed, Abbot Jacques of Amboise, built that gem of late-Gothic architecture, the Hotel de Cluny in Paris. The churches and clois-

ters of this old monastery richly deserve a visit and
then we may push on over the hills and mountains,

Roman Gateway, Autun

via Le Creusot, the flourishing and renowned Krupp
works, so to speak, of France to Autun.

Autun, we shall find to our surprise, still contains
extensive remains of the days when the city, then
known as Augustodunum, was a flourishing town of
the Roman Empire. Part of its walls and many of
its sixty towers still exist though much of them is
hidden among masses of foliage and modern buildings. But two of the most important gates still stand
in an excellent state of preservation. Each is pierced
by four arches, two larger ones for wheeled traffic and
two smaller ones for pedestrians and each is still surmounted by an arcaded gallery that connected the
ramparts at either side of the gate.

As one visits these and the other Roman remains
—the theatre, the so-called Temple of Janus and the
strange pyramid of masonry known as the Pierre de
Couhard—one realizes how the city has shrunk since
the days of Rome and now fills scarcely a third of the
circumference of its ancient walls. An excellent provincial inn boasts an historic room in which Napoleon
stayed, furnished to-day in pure Empire style as
when he occupied it.

THE AUSSOIS AND THE MORVAN

THE AUSSOIS AND THE MORVAN

I

SEMUR–EN–AUSSOIS

TO the west of Autun, rise the culminating peaks of the Morvan, that little Switzerland of central France, known to many a French family of summer vacationists but to few foreign travelers. Its peaks seldom pass an altitude of three thousand feet but seem higher, for they rise in a wild and rugged country, deeply mined by watercourses and clothed with thick woods and extensive pasture-lands over whose rocky wastes roam flocks of sheep and herds of cattle. The Morvandiaux are a strange, primitive-looking people said to be direct descendants of the Huns who remained in the country after the retreat of Attila's armies.

It is through this picturesque region that our road now lies, via Saulieu, with its fine old twelfth-century church (a foretaste of what we shall see at Avallon and Vezelay) and Precy-sous-Thil, dominated by the imposing ruins of its castle, to Semur.

Semur-en-Aussois, from whichever angle it is approached, is bound to be a surprise. For, traversing the surrounding country from any direction over broad plateaux of stubble-fields, bordered to the north by isolated table-like mountains, one is little prepared for the first sight of Semur, sitting high above the profound and narrow gorge that has been worn through the ages by the Armançon, a river that almost completely enfolds the city in its watery embrace. This wild and picturesque gorge owes its chief beauty to the remarkable size and ardent color of the red, granitic rocks, spangled with mica and quartz, that form its walls and have supplied the building material for the ramparts and massive towers, the terraced garden walls and the houses that surmount them, so that, whether you view this gorge from above, and watch the river, far below, threading its meanders through groves of poplars; or, from below, look up at the city perched high above you upon its ruddy walls of living stone, the site becomes one of the most striking in France.

And man, instead of detracting by his work (as is,

Semur

alas, too often the case) has added greatly to its splendor, for the bastions and battlemented walls and towers of its vast donjon, the delicate towers of its parish church and the huddle of the houses along the brink of its precipices, add greatly to the picture.

And when one begins to explore the hidden recesses of its twisting streets, one discovers new interest at every turn. Viollet-le-Duc cites its Church of Notre Dame as a chef-d'œuvre of the best period of Gothic architecture, "pour son execution si belle et l'admirable entente de son mode de construction." Its niches and portals are still adorned with many statues that may well be compared with the most elegant that the thirteenth century produced. The immense towers of the Donjon take on a new majesty at close range, and as Viollet-le-Duc also declares, cracked as they are with long fissures that zigzag from top to bottom, they will still live forever if left to the ravages of time alone. Then there is a splendid medieval city-gate, the Porte Sauvigny; there are quantities of quaint and picturesque old houses in the narrow, twisting streets and a number, too, of handsome private *hotels* (for, during the eighteenth century, Semur was the abode of provincial families of distinction) along its outer rim, that command beautiful views of the gorge below and of all the surrounding country.

Alas, today, there is no public hotel worthy of mention, and this is a pity, for Semur would otherwise be a delightful place in which to linger, not only to enjoy the old city itself but, from it, to visit the places of interest near by.

Only a few miles distant, for example, is the hill, the Mont Aussois or Auxois, upon which Vercingetorix made his last stand against the conquering legions of Cæsar. A great statue of the Gallic hero now crowns this hill and is visible for miles around.

Traces of the lines of circumvallation and contrevallation, marking the trenches dug by the Roman legionnaires have lately been unearthed by enterprising archæologists and recent excavations have also brought to light extensive remains of the Gallo-Roman city of Alesia: theatre, a temple, colonnaded edifices, a forum and an entire Gallic quarter, as well as débris of architecture and sculpture, sarcophagi, inscriptions, moneys, objects in bronze, bone, iron, wood and glass, all of which are now brought together in the Musée Alesia half-way up the hill in the village of Alise-Sainte-Reine, named for the virgin martyr, Sainte Reine, whose shrine attracts thousands of pilgrims annually.

One may prolong a visit to Alesia by continuing on over the plains to Bussy-le-Grand, a village dominated by a château rendered famous by Roger de Bussy-Rabutin, a cousin of Madame de Sevigné, who was exiled here by Louis XIV because, in his "Histoire Amoureuse des Gaules," he had twitted and lampooned the King and members of his court.

As you ascend the winding road from the hamlet below, you can spy no hint of the château until all of a sudden, you are upon it and see its gray façades and its moat filled with water reflecting its four cylindrical towers. Its court of honor is square and spacious but faces a dark and mysterious park, peopled with magnificent trees, centuries old, whose pendant branches touch the earth. Mossy flights of steps lead to sombre avenues that end in darkness and this darksome park and quiet château make one think of the Sleeping Beauty, dormant under the spell of a magician's wand. The castle really has a very remote mood, far from any town or human activity.

Roger de Rabutin, Comte de Bussy, a cultivated

gentleman, to lessen the mortal ennui of the seventeen years of his exile, began the collections that now grace the handsome rooms. He specialized in portraits and particularly in portraits of the ladies of the court of his time, venting his spleen upon them by having rather venomous inscriptions painted upon their frames, thus: "La Comtesse d'Olonne, la plus belle femme de son temps, mais moins célèbre par son beauté que par l'usage qu'elle en fit"; "Isabelle de Montmorency, a laquelle on ne pouvait réfuser ni sa bourse, ni son cœur, mais qui ne faisait pas cas de la bagatelle," etc. In the Salle des Devises, he painted a series of panels—sort of acidulous, allegorical pictures composed to revenge himself upon poor Madame de Montglas, who deserted him after his disgrace. His own portrait, a handsome canvas by Lebrun, hangs over the chimney-piece.

There are other things in the castle worthy of note. There is the chamber that Madame de Sevigné occupied with its canopied bed and its pictures by Greuze and Mignard; there is the Salon des Hommes de Guerre, panelled in wood and decorated with sixty odd effigies of celebrated military commanders, among whom Bussy-Rabutin himself figures, with becoming modesty, as erstwhile Lieutenant-General of the King's forces. There is also the Tour Dorée, a great, circular room in one of the corner towers, panelled and richly gilded and decorated with portraits and allegorical compositions and, finally, there is the long gallery of the Kings of France with portraits of all the French Kings from the Merovingians to the Bourbons, so that these artistic riches scattered so bounteously throughout the château make of Bussy-Rabutin a veritable museum.

Upon the other side of Semur, on the road that connects it with Avallon, lies the old town of Epoisses with a fine collegiate church and a remarkable feudal castle that forms a *pendant,* as it were, to Bussy. The key to the valley, its massive walls were built in the fourteenth century and have withstood some celebrated sieges. They were further strengthened, two hundred years later, by the double set of walls and moats that still encircle it today, and the château, in its exterior façades, has retained the grim walls of a medieval fortress.

But its Cour d'Honneur is gay and smiling. Above the entrance-door is an escutcheon, bearing upon its quarterings, some dice, which commemorate, if I remember rightly, the passing of the château from one member of the family to another upon a throw of dice. But Epoisses, in all the years of its existence, has never been sold, the ancestors of the present owner, the Comte de Guitaut, having occupied it continuously since the twelfth century.

Like its neighbor, Bussy-Rabutin, Epoisses has its gallery of portraits of Princes, warriors, and celebrated men, including the four great Dukes of Burgundy: Charles le Temeraire, Jean le Bon, Jean sans Peur, and Philippe le Hardi. The billiard-room is ornamented with long lines of ancestral portraits of the Guitaut family and in the center of the antichamber is a magnificent suit of knight's armor given by Marshal Soult to his grand-daughter, the Comtesse de Guitaut of her day. Epoisses has also its "chambre de Madame de Sevigné," richly furnished and hung with superb tapestries, and among the Château's most prized possessions, preserved in its archives in a special tower, are the autograph letters written by the Marquise de Sevigné to her dear friends, the Guitauts of her time.

II

AVALLON AND VEZELAY

ONLY a few miles separate Epoisses from
Avallon, the town of the region that is best
fitted for a stay. Not that Avallon itself is
more interesting than the other towns, but from it,
some very charming excursions can be made, and it
contains at least one hostelry where the tourist can be
comfortably housed.

Avallon's newer quarters are bright and busy; its
outer boulevards are broad and shaded by fine trees
and it boasts, I think, one of the best World War
monuments in France—a massive poilu, strong and
heavily equipped for trench duty standing in a quiet
but resolute pose over a fallen comrade. Behind this
group, the names of Avallon's dead (and how many
there are!) are inscribed upon the faces of four simple pillars that support an entablature.

The principal square is named in honor of Avallon's most distinguished son, Vauban, the great mili-

tary engineer. Adjoining it is a handsome promenade shaded by enormous pleached chestnut-trees. From it too, the Grande Rue leads into the older quarters of the town, where are some quaint old Gothic houses and a few fine residences such as the Hôtel Condé, to which the Grand Condé used to come, from time to time, to breathe the sweet, clean air of the Morvan.

A little farther on, the Grande Rue terminates at the Tour de l'Horloge, an old belfry or clock-tower, that bestrides the street, which, beyond this point, is known as the Rue Bocquillot. Its character, too, changes with its name, for it now becomes even more like a medieval thoroughfare bordered by turreted houses and venerable churches.

One of these, the Church of Saint Lazare, is particularly worthy of notice, being, indeed, the chief artistic lion of Avallon. Rebuilt, upon a still older church, in the twelfth century, it offers a highly interesting specimen of Romanesque architecture, its two west portals being unusually fine examples of this style, with their twisted and fluted columns and their archivolts richly adorned with garlands of fruits and flowers. Its interior also is picturesque and curious,

The Cours Vauban, Avallon

the main floor of the nave dropping, by means of steps, to lower levels, until, when the altar is reached, one is more than ten feet below the street level.

Beyond this church, you pass through the city walls, still guarded by their *echauguettes* or corner watch-towers, and issue, by means of the Petite Porte, upon a shady esplanade that commands a beautiful and far-reaching panorama—a view that, certainly to my mind, constitutes the chief attraction of Avallon. Deep down below you is a wild and narrow valley, worn through the centuries by the waters of the Cousin, a little river that often ripples into rapids and foaming cascades. Beyond this valley, the hills of the Morvan, forest-clad, stretch to a far horizon, apparently uncultivated and dotted only here and there with a château or a residence.

There are some delightful excursions to be made into this Morvan region. There are the seamed and rugged rocks of Pierre-Perthuis, pierced by caves and natural arches; there is the fine old castle of Chastellux with its six battlemented towers overlooking its park and gardens; there is the Benedictine monastery of Sainte-Marie-de-la-Pierre-qui-Vire, built in a savage solitude of granite boulders and dominating the

[225]

banks of the Trinquelin, one of the enormous stones, the Pierre-qui-Vire or Turning Stone, from which the monastery takes its name, being surmounted by a great statue of the Virgin.

But the excursion from Avallon that no one can afford to miss is that to Vezelay.

The direct road passes Pontaubert, still in the valley of the Cousin, then ascends over a succession of hills, to Fontette, whence it drops again into the pretty valley of the Cure. We first reach Saint Père-sous-Vezelay, a primitive village, where, if you search about a bit among its tortuous lanes, malodorous with dung-heaps, you will find the remarkable church of Saint Père. Its rather florid porch is later than the church itself, which is pure thirteenth-century Gothic and is still surmounted by a very tall tower, elegant in proportions and picturesque in design, with story upon story of superposed arches adorned with saints and trumpet-blowing angels.

Beyond Saint Père you begin to mount a long hill, with fascinating glimpses, as you go, of Vezelay perched high above you on its hilltop, its walls, towers, tiled-roofed houses and church spires piling up in picturesque confusion. You finally stop in a broad sort of open space that is usually the ultimate goal of wheeled traffic, though an automobile can make its way farther up the single, narrow street of the town.

La Porte Neuve, Vezelay

I prefer, however, to walk. First of all, because I like to look over at the Inn of the White Horse that fronts upon this *place* and think of the many long-haired young men and short-haired young women who have kept their paint boxes and canvasses in its

[227]

clean and homelike rooms and some of whom will usually be found sitting about its doorway or sketching in the vicinity.

Then I like leisurely to saunter up the long street that ascends abruptly toward the Church of Mary Magdalen, whose façade one spies, from time to time, blocking the vista at the end of the street. Along the way are many quaint old houses, among them one that thrills me whenever I see it. It is a modest affair that has been done over at different periods but still retains an early-Gothic doorway above which is an inscription. This tablet informs us that this humble dwelling, once a part of the Infirmary, housed Louis VII, called Le Jeune, when he passed through Vezelay on his way to the Second Crusade, which Saint Bernard here preached in March, 1146. What a picture this all brings to mind—a picture whose interest is further enhanced when one remembers that it was at Vezelay also that Philip Augustus and Richard Cœur de Lion assumed the Cross about a hundred and forty years later.

Souvenirs such as these put us in a fitting mood to approach the venerable Church of La Madeleine which crowns the hill and is visible for many miles around. Its exterior is stern and grim, as befits a Crusaders' church, with little ornament or decoration to mitigate its plain surfaces. It proves, however, upon closer scrutiny, to be one of the most interesting pieces of ecclesiastical architecture in France, thoroughly restored (perhaps too much so) about a century ago by Viollet-le-Duc.

If possible, you should enter it by the west door (which is usually locked) through the narthex, one of the largest and most imposing that I have ever seen, and in which, we are told, the faithful were allowed to sleep upon the floor during the great pilgrimages. It is elaborately and magnificently decorated with sculptured ornament and many figures, particularly the portal that connects it with the church beyond. If you can induce the guardian to open this portal you will be richly rewarded, for, through it, and with it as a foreground, you obtain a superb view of the lofty nave beyond.

I can recall no finer picture of twelfth-century church architecture than this vista in the church of Vezelay. And when one examines more closely the details of each arch and capital, of each archivolt and corbel, one is amazed at the beauty of the sculptured ornament, the figures, both large and small, the capitals of infinite variety, the richness of the foliations completing an ensemble of almost unique beauty.

The grassy terraces that surround this church command far-reaching panoramas in all directions, and the loveliness of the country tempts one to linger, especially toward evening, when the sun gilds all with a ruddy glaze, until darkness comes.

To the northward, the eye follows the undulations of the valley of the Cure, up the meanders of which lies our shortest and prettiest route to Paris, past Arcy-sur-Cure and the rocky cliffs of Cravant to Auxerre, whose many spired churches overlook the peaceful Yonne. Thence on to Paris is an easy and evident route—and thus will end our little tour "Through the French Provinces."